Black Liberation through Action and Resistance

Black Liberation through Action and Resistance

MOVE

Frederick V. Engram Jr.

HAMILTON BOOKS
AN IMPRINT OF
ROWMAN & LITTLEFIELD
Lanham • Boulder • New York • London

Published by Hamilton Books
An imprint of The Rowman & Littlefield Publishing Group, Inc.
4501 Forbes Boulevard, Suite 200, Lanham, Maryland 20706
www.rowman.com

86-90 Paul Street, London EC2A 4NE, United Kingdom

British Library Cataloguing in Publication Information Available

Library of Congress Cataloging-in-Publication Data Available

ISBN 9780761874164 (pbk.) | ISBN 9780761874171 (ebook)

Tracklist

Preface

One of my most common phrases that I tweet a few times a month is *y'all don't hate white supremacy enough for me*. I often say this because through my years in education and doing critical race work, I have come to realize that at the most foundational level many of us have no idea what white supremacy *actually* is or how deadly it can be. As a Black millennial and a descendant of the enslaved Africans brought to this country, I believe that I am poised to understand various perspectives of this journey and where the educational gaps exist, need nudging, and or a complete redirection. Consider this work a calling-in, a tight hug, a shoulder tap, and a redirection.

A HUMBLE REQUEST

As far as the United States of America has come in regard to race relations it still has not gone far enough. Every news cycle there is a story about an elected state official, an elected federal official, and everyday people spreading misinformation about the power [*or dismissal of it*] of racism, white supremacy, anti-Black racism, and misogynoir. As a person who is in the weeds doing the work of re-educating people and teaching people how to be critical thinkers, I often find myself enraged and heartbroken about the insistence of slavery and its remnants as inconsequential to the contemporary American story. African Americans are perpetually gaslit into believing that our stories are false, race baiting, or ahistorical, and we have had enough. This work is for those of who know and are learning that resistance is *not* a one-time occurrence. I pray that this piece is a conversation starter not a conversation book end. Black liberation is the responsibility of us all! Put on your sensible shoes and get to work, I'll meet you there.

Acknowledgments

This book would not be possible if not for my engaging with Black Twitter! Before the car guy took over, Black Twitter provided an outlet for so many non-white scholars and non-scholars alike to gather and exist without all of the pretenses of the academy. If it were not for my connections to both Minda Harts and Dr. Jesse Daniels liking and retweeting my tweets my meeting Emi Ikkanda would not have been possible. Thank you, Emi for assisting me in getting my thoughts about *Black liberation* and *misogynoir* into proposal form. Thank you!

Several members of my personal community listened to me and my thoughts at different stages of my writing process and I am thankful to you all for doing so! Especially for those of you who took my calls during the wee-hours of the night and morning and or provided feedback. This is not an exhaustive list, but it is my most reoccurring cast of characters: My dear sister *Zaquoiyah*, my homies *Justin A.*, and *Dr. Kabugi*, my Pham/sister-friend *Asia*, My mom, my dear friend *Candace W.*, and *Dr. Kandace H.* Thank you all! Your patience and thoughts helped me to keep myself centered in what this work is purposed for—*Us!*

To my neo–*Isaac L* for taking my vision for my book cover and bringing it to life! I know that it was a tremendous undertaking for you, but I hope you know how appreciative of you I always am. You are a true talent, and you have the patience of Job! I love you, bro! From House 36, to DC, to our 100th Centennial, and beyond!

Thank you to Brooke Bures at Rowman & Littlefield for giving my first book baby a soft place to land. Thank you to the editorial staff, marketing staff, and everyone involved in making sure this work could see the light of day!

I will forever honor my grandmothers in all that I do. To you Grandma Anna (*R.I.P.*) and to you Grandma Laura, cheers!

Chapter 1

Stand Up

Black Liberation for Black People and Co-Conspirators

In the movie *Harriet* starring Cynthia Erivo, Erivo uses her mezzo-soprano voice to encourage the enslaved to *Stand Up*. She does this by encouraging them all to trust in the Lord's plan for their liberation and that she with the Lord's oversight would be their guide. The work of liberation is work that should encompass everyone since oppression is a system that includes everyone. However, many Americans do not feel that liberatory work is their responsibility. Particularly liberation work that involves giving more access to the descendants of the formerly enslaved. America has a very unique way of providing access and support for white people who have been *othered* in their homelands. While simultaneously pretending to be obtuse to the very racist living condition that befalls American citizens who happen to be racialized as Black. There have been countless examples of African Americans experiencing the worst of this country while America tells this particular class of people to wait. Wait on laws to protect their right to vote; ability to make reproductive decisions; to be openly and proudly queer; or to walk down the street and to drive a car without fear of death at the hands of those sworn to protect and serve. As Beyoncé says, *America has a problem!*

THE PROBLEM

America has long been seated in the throne of judgement. Through the lens of our American-ness we often view other countries and nations in this world as less than. The obvious success of white supremacy is that it has created the idea that anything not equal to or greater than America is worthless or requires a forced redirection. Americans view European countries as a standard of

1

what life and living should be like while also looking at African nations as something to be disgusted by. The standard of beauty is often viewed through a lens of whiteness or whitewashed Black appropriation. Whitewashed Black appropriation is what caused countless mainstream white women to pad their bottom regions, slick their hair back, wear large hoop earrings, tan their bodies, and increase the size of their lips while it was popular. Before ultimately running back to whiteness and its privileges. For it is more beneficial to appropriate Blackness than it actually is to be Black and a woman. To have a sense of what is required for us to liberate ourselves we have to first discuss and interrogate the parts of ourselves that white supremacy has corrupted. Whether it be arguing about which Black people are worthy of liberation or feeling that as a Black person you need to defend *"the good white people."* We are *ALL* affected by the stain of enslavement upon this nation and the white supremacy that was created as a result of the construction of race and ultimately the racialized hierarchy.

The creation of whiteness as a legal framework from which America bases its foundation is damning in both theory and in practice. The founding fathers never once considered an America where the enslaved were liberated or considered fully human. Any idea of originalism or being a constitutionalist without being a strict critic of both and a proponent of their restructuring quite simply means that your beliefs and values are rooted in racism. America is quite literally a failed social experiment hanging on by a thread because the old guard (*cishet, white, wealthy, male, elected officials*) refuse to either die or reimagine a world where the most marginalized among us are no longer held there by legislation and systemic loopholes aimed at benefiting whiteness. America ran away from the crown only to become obsessed by it and judging those who will not bend the knee and turn the other cheek in regard to their imperialism, incest, and genocide. America is obsessed with the idea of subjugation and stratification of individuals based on the qualities assigned to the white and privileged. This practice has long existed and constantly shows its face when one least expects. No member of any marginalized group in this country is safe, *anywhere!* White supremacy is so crafty that it even offers stratification to the oppressed. Any oppressed category that white persons can fall into will automatically place their suffering ahead of any category that solely applies to Blackness. For these reasons, it is important that we remove the mask that Paul Laurence Dunbar referred to. The time of our asking with weighted brow and heavy hearts has long passed, it is time that we demand. The success of white supremacy is that it has us [*the marginalized*] at odds about what those demands should look like and who should be centered in them. All of this is wrong because there should be no stratification in regard to our liberation. The act of liberation means pushing forward and resisting so that all of the children under the reign of white supremacy, racism, and anti-Blackness are free at once.

White supremacy is successful because it has made many of us believe that the favor that we have with the system of whiteness makes us inherently better. It is this perspective that makes many of us feel high and mighty and above our brothers and sisters who are struggling a bit more than we are. It is the same positionality that allows you to believe that *broke people* chose their life. Instead of questioning the system that constructed poverty and it being directly connected to the school-to-prison pipeline, we question each other's financial decisions. The sheer number of financial literacy gurus who take aim at teaching the marginalized how to control their spending and to be better stewards of their savings all while not acknowledging white supremacy as your greatest debt. You cannot out-save, outwit, or outlast a system designed to come for you at every turn without first acknowledging the grip that it has on all of our existence. Through the years, I have heard the respectable Black folks counter [with the tired trope] that wealth is our way out of racism. There is no dollar amount, no position of authority, no skin tone, and no secret circle that will protect you from the reign of terror that is white supremacy. However, understanding what we are dealing with will equip us with the tools that we all need to *stand up* and fight back!

THE RIGHT AND THE WOKE

Black liberation has always been an act of political warfare between the oppressed and those who wish to see us shackled, both in theory and in practice. The politics of freedom were never a conversation that was intended to happen. When the white men who founded this country began writing the constitution for this stolen land it was not a conceivable thought that those who they enslaved would one day vote, hold office, or be elected President of these United States. We were never intended to be considered fully human or to have a voice in politics or elsewhere. When right-wing politicians use the term *American* to describe the people of this land, the white is always silent. African Americans are never truly considered in their conversation and are only ever considered when pawns for political propaganda are needed. As we look at the 2022 midterm candidates across the nation there have been strategically selected Black people who were never political hopefuls who were tapped by the far right. The intention is not to provide a voice for the historically marginalized. The intent is to provide a narrative that African Americans do not vote based on logic or practical things like policing, taxes, or healthcare but that we vote solely based on Blackness, and this perspective is rooted in anti-Black racism. To believe that African Americans are not and have not always been politically astute is the work of white supremacy. As the descendants of the formerly enslaved in this country every move that we make is rooted in politics. Where we live, what schools we attend, how we talk or code-switch, how we navigate this world is all politics. Politics of identity and the politics of survival since we do not have the freedom to navigate this world as privileged, obtuse, or naïve individuals. Only white children are allowed to grow up in a world where they can choose when to opt-in to politics and based on issues of being pro-liberation or pro-oppression. It is also why apolitical white people are more problematic than many of them choose to believe.

As a person of racialized privilege, it is your responsibility to take part in the causes that fight for liberation if you indeed consider yourself to be anti-racist. Many white Americans feel that simply stating that they are not racist or have never uttered the n-word is sufficient enough to grant them their anti-racist certification. Fortunately, being considered anti-racist is more than performative verbiage aimed at centering whiteness like most DEI initiatives. To be considered anti-racist it requires of you to give up something and it is one of your first steps on your journey to being a co-conspirator (Love 2020). As Bettina Love often states, being a co-conspirator is a step above simply being an ally. For me, being an ally is on brand for people who still center whiteness in DEI initiatives. Being an ally is still passive in most arenas because it allows for the person in proximity to the oppression to decide *if* they should assist. There is no real requirement for them to get involved but it still allows them to claim anti-racist and ally status. Being a co-conspirator requires for you to become physically, emotionally, mentally, spiritually, and financially invested. It quite literally requires of you to use your prestige and class as a person racialized as white to advance equity for the marginalized and to disrupt your own privilege for the benefit of others. Allyship allows you to sit in your place of privilege while deciding who among the oppressed is deserving of your saving, which inherently still seats you in the role of oppressor. Most people who use the term ally or see themselves as allies are also people who still look at certain members of minoritized groups as inferior even if they never say the words aloud. They still believe that people should look and act a certain way in order to be worthy of liberating. These individuals are what some might consider *anti-racist-racists* as indicated by Kohli, Pizarro, and Nevárez in their 2017 published article about *The New Racism*.

America constantly shows minoritized members of society that accountability and making people whole is something that they're unwilling to do. The mere mention of reparations of any sort is met with immediate vitriol and anti-Blackness. America as a political system is not as equity minded as people are expected to believe. Regardless of what each party espouses as the core of their "causes," the majority of their elected members do not wish to truly support Black liberation. It is impossible to be pro-police, pro-incarceration, and pro-poverty and claim to be anti-racist or truly equity centered. Politics on both sides of the aisle do not truly align with liberation and that is why the liberals and conservatives are more alike than they are different. The political campaigns waged at dismembering *woke-ism* are simply political attacks aimed at the more marginalized among us.

The media uses its long reach to pick and choose which elements of particular stories are worth telling. Any stories aimed at uplifting or bringing awareness to the stories of the marginalized are being tied to wokeness. Right-wing politicians and the media use "woke" as a catch all for all things inherently Black and or liberatory. America is rooted in white supremacy and by the social construction of race by default, racism. Pretending that the very present qualities of these United States are not entrenched in keeping the *haves* and the *have-nots* as separate and feuding classes is obtuse. America by design and because Americans refuse to address systems of inequity in full, reaps the benefits of both poverty and crime. Policing as a construct has never been for the prevention of crime. Policing of impoverished communities is solely for the purpose of finding ways to criminalize those who reside in redlined areas. Areas that they have been forced to reside in with little to no access or opportunity to exist. When an individual who finds some measure of ability to escape these areas, they are still oppressed by them simply because their families still likely reside there.

UNDERSTANDING WHITE PRIVILEGE

White people struggle with the concept of privilege because they automatically associate the idea of privilege with wealth, property, and success or the assumption of each. For most white people they have not had to wrestle with their identity or how they show up in the world because of it along with the consequences of it. Whiteness is the cloak that provides safety from these experiences as well as the blindfold that prevents seeing themselves in similar circumstances. For white people who have not disrupted their relationship with whiteness the mere idea that they have possession of any unearned privileges would send them into a crisis. This response is because white people have been told since birth that everything in the world that they could ever dream of could be their own. Boundaries or the possibility of being denied something that they desire is not a fathomable concept. To them [white people] they do not see themselves as having an unfair advantage gifted to them solely on the basis of their racialized hierarchal category. For them [white people] anything that they desire to have is simply a matter of working hard enough for it. For Black folks, even when we meet all of the requirements for any given thing, we doubt ourselves. White supremacy has caused there to always be a shadow of a doubt placed on anything that Black folks legitimately earn. The deficit framed belief system is constantly placed upon Black children in schools as they interact with ill-prepared teachers, administrators, and school counselors. As an example, when a Black student states that they want to attend a top school and they are advised that they should consider a junior college or a state school only. There is nothing wrong with either of those two options, but there is privilege in that white students are not often counseled in the same manner. White privilege allows for white children to grow up never being told what to do if they encounter racism, the police, or a random neighbor pretending to be an authority. The idea of white children having their space policed is only ever a conversation when it pertains to teaching real history and school board meetings.

White children who then become white adults are not relegated to having to constantly be aware of how much space they take up, who they can engage with or date, and where they can work or live. This is white privilege. If you as a white person have never had "the talk" regarding what to do if an officer stops you, you have white privilege. If as a white person you have not ever worried about being put out of school because your hair was too long or too colorful, you have white privilege. If you have not ever considered shortening your name on your resume or CV or coming up with a westernized name, you have white privilege. Although these are just a few examples of what white privilege looks like, the concept is the same and that is that the privilege of whiteness has nothing to do with wealth or monetary items possessed as an individual. Whiteness and its privileges are directly related because of the system that allows each of them to flourish, unchecked and unchallenged. White privilege is the very thing boiling up in your spirit that has you wanting to send angry e-mails or nastygrams because whiteness was mentioned.

Most people have not heard that race itself is a social construct that came into existence because Europeans wanted to create a racialized hierarchy that only allowed access for those deemed worthy. The creation of white as a race was also a patriarchal tool aimed at keeping European women on a very short leash regarding whom they could marry and have sex with. Anti-miscegenation was the law of the land, but it only applied to white women and non-white men [*namely the enslaved Africans and those indigenous to America*]. Anti-miscegenation laws did not stop white males from raping enslaved African women and creating forced births. European immigrants who entered America *after* the establishment of white as a race were also minoritized. They were berated, castigated, beaten, and taken through the ringer until they assimilated into whiteness. The descendants of many of the European groups that were forced into or accepted whiteness as a means of surviving this new world are likely unaware of it, yet they will defend being white. America never embraced the concept of pluralism which would allow for unique groups to exist in America freely and without forced assimilation.

This concept by many was believed to be one that would have naturally occurred partnerships and interconnectedness between the different groups. Instead, white Americans forced everyone into being *Anglo-Conformist* or measured against it in every possible way. America fought for her freedom just so she could adopt the same oppressive tactics of Great Britain in the name of patriotism and whiteness. Here is a controversial but truthful take and that is, being white is a choice. European Americans have the unique opportunity to simply reclaim who they are and denounce the entire system of whiteness and its benefits. Having this unique ability is also a privilege because it is something uniquely available to European Americans in a way that it is not available for African Americans. European Americans [white people] are not disconnected from their language or from their culture and a great number of them still have an elder or did have an elder who does or did things like cook in the "old way." Being able to directly connect to your relatives in your homeland is a benefit directly related to whiteness. If the majority of African Americans returned to Africa, most of us would not know where to begin in our search for biological relatives. The fact that we have to take ancestry tests to figure out where in Africa we descend from is proof positive of the violence and privilege of whiteness. Unless you are a white person in America who was adopted and not raised by anyone in your biological family you know who you are.

A defining characteristic of white privilege is that its beneficiaries are in most instances unaware of its power. Being unaware or pretending to be obtuse is necessary for white privilege to persist. You are probably wondering how they are "allegedly" unaware of their white authority, but they still manage to act like they own the place, right? This dynamic exists because as children, white people are not often taught to yield any space. White parents often provide rationalizations for why their children are deserving of any and all things and that any denial of said privilege is an affront to their existence. Think about the times you witnessed Johnny on the playground being unruly as hell. Where was his mother? She was likely not far away and either too busy to notice or she saw nothing wrong with her child's problematic behavior. The uninterrupted ideology of space-taking continued throughout Johnny's development and as he grew older, he began taking up more space. If anyone challenged the space that Johnny was taking up, his parents were there to rationalize and support him. Johnny then continued to move through life unchallenged or protected from challenge and eventually attends college. In college depending on where Johnny enrolls, he might meet his first obstacle that challenges his core belief system or what he had been raised to believe. A challenge that decenters Johnny and forces him to see the world not from the aspect of his unearned space-taking but one of yielding space and allowing others to exist. Johnny then has a decision to make for himself and likely it's the first time he has had to make this decision. Should he open himself up to interrogate what he was taught by his parents and begin the process of unlearning and relearning, or should he buck back? Based on the trajectory of Johnny's life up until this point he is most likely preparing to buck back. Bucking back is what white people do when their core belief system [*the one that centers them*] is threatened by audacity. The audacity to tell a white person that the world does in fact not revolve around them or that perhaps they should take up less space so that the marginalized might have a seat, is world ending. Not in the sense of a physical death but in the sense of a philosophical death.

White people are not often met with boundaries in America. Whether they are boundaries of the physical, mental, or emotional sense each of them are unfamiliar to whiteness and persons racialized as white. As a result of Johnny's being raised through and into privilege, he is likely incapable of seeing the world from a vantage point of the marginalized. As Johnny matriculates through college and he then enrolls into graduate school he will further cement his perspectives and belief systems. His belief system as a privileged cishet white male in America is only further cemented as he engages with others who identify the same way that he does. As a white person who considers themselves to be an ally, an accomplice, or a co-conspirator it is important to understand how you measure up against the Johnny's of the world. It is important to understand how those same principles and ideologies reside deep within you and require intentional and meaningful disruption. One cannot simply jump from the racialized category of being white and then call themselves an anti-racist. You must do the lifelong work of disassociating from the aspects of American life that uphold your privilege while subjugating others.

DISRUPTING WHITE PRIVILEGE

Johnny is an example of white maleness in America and what uninterrupted privilege can create. However, to his family and the people that revere him, Johnny *IS* America! He is quite literally what the framers envisioned when they began their constructing of this social experiment. The white women who were born to run counter to Johnny were not intended to inherit the earth in the same way that he was. White women were always viewed as an aside and a commodity for the Johnnie's of the world. The creation of whiteness and the subsequent creation of patriarchy post-Bacon's Rebellion was intended to pull mutual or individual autonomy away from women racialized as white. White women were no longer allowed to decide who they would engage in sexual intercourse with or marry if they planned to maintain their status as *white*. You are probably thinking to yourself, *"what the hell is Bacon's Rebellion?!"* and I am glad that you asked. Bacon's Rebellion began in 1676 and raged until 1677 in Jamestown, Virginia. Yes, the same Jamestown where twenty Africans arrived on the shores fifty-seven years prior, in 1619 un-enslaved.

As per the typical European concept of take what you please and call it your own, the colonists in Jamestown pushed back (Blakemore 2019). Nathaniel Bacon who was the marital cousin of colonial governor William Berkeley was what can be called a menace. He like many European people during those times [*similar to white people of today*] was willing to lie and cheat if it meant having his way. In the winter of 1676 Bacon attacked a native tribe that was considered "friendly" and accused the tribe of stealing his corn (Blakemore 2019). Remember that it was the natives who introduced corn to the colonizers in the first place so this declaration would ring rather odd for most. Bacon demanded that he be afforded a militia to attack the natives who bordered the colony, and his request was denied. As a result of his request being denied and based upon his entitlement as a colonizer, Bacon assembled his own militia which included other native persons (Occaneechi) and Black Virginians (Blakemore 2019). Bacon would later turn on the Occaneechi and then destroy their lands as well. As a result of such an audacious move by Black Virginians along with poor and struggling Europeans, their action began to plant seeds for a need to divide and conquer the rebellious groups. The tool that was used to divide and conquer these groups was the intentional creation of *race*. Race at its inception was intended to be a tool of division. When you hear folks make this repetitive argument, *"Why does everything have to be about race?"* you can let them know that the creation of race and racism are core and legal as foundational to the running of America. Race and racism were also the core components of chattel slavery in the colonies. Race is and has always been a tool for subjugation and necessary for dominant and minoritized group relations.

A necessary task that a white person who is looking to move toward anti-racism and the support for Black liberation, is to understand the afore-mentioned as foundational to the story. Anti-racism cannot be achieved without first knowing how race and subsequently racism were created and understanding why they are successful. Jumping into the role of a co-con-spirator, accomplice, or ally without first understanding how your whiteness blinds you and how your relationship with it may keep you from ever truly being in support of Black liberation. There must be a full and complete dis-ruption of your participation in oppressive norms where you decide who is worthy of your good deeds. Recognizing that the most marginalized among the oppressed are not going to be the people who often make you the most comfortable. The most disproportionately impacted by oppression are not always going to be your soft spoken, well put-together, easy to communicate with, and most accepting of your presence in their space types. Even when they are less than welcoming of your presence and space-taking they are *still* deserving of liberation. The natural inclination is to reject those who reject you but that is not an opportunity that you as a member of the dominant class have in this instance. Considering that African Americans are always gaslit about our experiences with oppression and or made promises that are not kept, it makes it easier to start at a place of mistrust and then gradually move toward being open and vulnerable. As a person who has committed their life to liberatory work you must understand that the bumps and bruises to your ego are par for the course. Those bumps and bruises also pale in comparison to what it means to be African American or Black and American.

BLACK RELIGIOSITY AND LIBERATION

One of the only things that African Americans had during enslavement and after was our relationship with religion. Black folks love their Lord, the church, and the pomp and circumstance that accompanies it. During enslavement it was one of the very few times where we were sometimes allowed to gather free of the white gaze. It was also a time where our ancestors were allowed to enact some of their very traditional and African-centered practices. The church was also a place of strategizing and heavy contemplation about what was to come and how to prepare for it. However, with many of the other attributes of the antebellum period we picked up quite a few anti-Black and anti-human sentiments.

As the years have passed on and generations have become more aware of ourselves and those whom we love, we have also become intolerant to hate. Not just the hate inflicted upon us at the hands of our oppressors, but also the hate inflicted upon us by those who claim to love us, our own people. I will be the first to admit that as I have aged as a millennial that my relationship with religion and spirituality have shifted significantly from the time since I was a child. I would venture to say that the same would apply to my siblings, cousins, friends, and peers. We were in church most Sundays, in the Easter pageants, and knew all of the rites and rituals that accompanied the African American Baptist experience. However, something began to shift for me, and that shift has a lot to do with contradictions between religion and liberation. *Stand up* as mentioned in the beginning of this chapter in regard to Erivo's signaling of the enslaved to flee can also be a rousing call to those aggrieved by religiosity and its juxtaposition to liberation. Church was once all that we had to hear our humble cries, but it has in many instances turned into the place of our spiritual deaths. Why? It is quite simple to explain if you ask me. Many of our spiritual leaders have not done the readings and it is present in their teachings and the harm caused to their congregations. In an article written by the Black Youth Project in 2019, the contributors raised the point that the spirituality of Black millennials is broadening, and we are beginning to resonate more with our ancestors and less with oppressive spaces. As mentioned in the article, Christian spaces have left millennials feeling that there was no refuge for us to thrive spiritually as well as worship (Black Youth Project 2019). The article further states that Black millennials are leaving in search of space and practices that are overtly inclusive of our ancestral practices, sexuality, and race (Black Youth Project 2019).

The Black Church was always supposed to be our place of refuge, healing, restoration, and enlightenment. The problem is that the Black Church in some respects has failed to grow alongside its parishioners. We see queerness in the choir and in the usher board members, but we also see and hear the pastor make comments like, *"God made Adam and Eve, not Adam and Steve!"* Well, who the hell made Steve then?! The Black Church and in certain instances Black culture has absolutely adopted white supremacy as a practice that we call religion. Religiosity in the American context is simply white supremacy with scriptures. The same scriptures that were used to subjugate our ancestors we now use to subjugate each other. *Stand up!*

As we begin to wrestle with our liberation and our spirituality, we are beginning to do the very thing that we are taught not to do in the Black Church and that is, *"Do not question God!"* I am pretty sure that the creator who sees and knows all things, sees, and knows that I had questions before I did! It is difficult to reconcile that a God who is just and on time would allow our people to suffer for as long as he has. We have witnessed other minoritized groups receive reparations and legislation aimed at minimizing unwarranted hateful attacks against them and we still wait. At what point are we justified in the asking of necessary questions? Is it at the pearly gates, on the way to the gates, once the gates close? When? Obviously, these are questions without immediate answers but how do you expect millennials who are with necessary inquiries to just do nothing? African American millennials, who are arguably among the most credentialed and educated in our families, are also more spiritually grounded than our peers in other racial groups (Collins 2018). Therefore, the idea of just allowing our questions to go unanswered or to be made to fill unfulfilled as we mimic the practices of our parents is simply not enough. The fleeing of African American millennials from the church is not new and has been happening amid political and cultural shifts over the last decade (Collins 2018). African American millennials are clashing with scripture-centered, patriarchal, anti-Black rhetoric (Collins 2018). We are choosing to focus on liberation in both the physical and spiritual sense. Our parents not being able to engage with us regarding our questions pertaining to both religion and liberation is a stalemate for many of us. Education which has been the greatest tool of liberation for African American millennials has taught us to think, critique, and critically examine the world and its many irregularities. We are fully aware of what is broken in religiosity and are curious to find a solution that works for us and our people regardless of it being a popular opinion and or not considered respectable.

As we further consider our relationships with religiosity and liberation we are marred by the constant blows of anti-Blackness and performance [shock] theology. Shock theology is also an aspect that exists today that does not directly speak to the current needs of millennials who are reckoning with oppression and spirituality. Creating shock worthy moments that go viral does not equate to liberation or soul saving work, in fact I would venture further to say that it is purely foolish. Womanist and Black Liberation theologies were often used to educate, empower, and equip congregants for collective and personal efficacy (Barnes 2006). These liberatory theologies allowed us to sit with how we could interpret scripture and how it could ultimately address oppressive issues at large, and inequities based upon race, sexual orientation, and gender (Barnes 2006). Why are Black Churches not wrestling with figuring out ways to bring these more precisely needed and accurate teachings to the center? The answer is short, and the answer is, *patriarchy*.

The Black Church use to be intentional about proactively identifying and addressing social problems like racism and poverty (Barnes 2006). What about also addressing the issues that members of the Black Church reinforce that directly run adjacent to white supremacy? Liberatory work has to also center the acknowledgment of practices that you yourself engage in that are the antithesis of pro-Black resistance and liberation. If your religious stance allows you to dismiss "certain" Black people because you do not agree with their position in life, you are doing liberation wrong. If Christianity according to Barnes (2006) is intended to be a mechanism for liberation, why does it seem and or feel depending on who you ask so oppressive? Black Liberation theology has ties to the Black consciousness movement of the 1960s and can be linked much earlier to the work of thinkers like David Walker (1829), Bishop Henry Turner in the late 19th century, and Kimpa Vita (1703) (Barnes 2006). Black religiosity's ties to Black liberation were necessary connections because it was what was required of our spiritual guides during that time. Have the children of the silent generation made that negative of an impact on how we combine church and our fight for liberation? I surely hope not but based upon the traditions and politics of respectability and those who reinforce it, it certainly appears that way.

One of the things that causes me to have a most visceral reaction are the politics of respectability and how the Black Church reinforces them. As we watch countless viral videos of my brothers all sharp and dressed to the nines posing for photos in front of the NMAAHC in Washington D.C. to Baltimore, Atlanta, and Los Angeles, I find myself conflicted. No one gets dressed to impress better than Black folks all over the diaspora, no one. I find myself conflicted because when some of those involved have been asked what is the purpose the response is often, *"we want to change the narrative."* What narrative exactly? The politics of respectability forced down upon us first from whiteness and then the Black Church forces us to believe that we [the oppressed] are the issue. That if we just look the part and look like we have somewhere important to be that somehow, just maybe, racism will escape us.

The conflict for me is more aligned with how both the poor and working-class Black folks are expected to comport themselves into the ideal image of Blackness that would be satisfactory to the white gaze (Gray 2016; Harris 2003).

As a result of some of these same thought processes and teachings we often see Black women made small and minimized in the fight for liberation as if Black women have not always been the main organizers from the Civil Rights Movement to the Black Lives Matter Movement. Recognizing that Black women are pivotal to our advancement in Black liberatory work and resistance is crucial (Harris 2003). Especially Black women who are both queer and loud! Part of African American millennial resistance of where the Black Church currently sits is largely connected to its political positioning and respectability therein. There is a reason millennials cheered when President Biden and his administration began fighting back against the spread of misinformation via the White House social media page. We have been waiting for the elders to get on board and to join us in whatever capacity they can, not to continue telling us to simply be quiet. Millennials often get a bad rap. We are blamed for all of the misdeeds of Generation X and the mayhem of Generation Z without proper credit given to the things that we are actually doing, like raising our families and continuing the fight for liberation. The responsibility with how Black people are seen in the world amid our oppression is placed at our feet. Since the initial goal of racial uplift drove the cultural politics of respectability we have long been tasked with puttin forth our best *Black* self (Gray 2016). Considering the fact that we are aware that regardless of how we look we can still be killed it has always puzzled me when folks say things like, *"She is making us all look bad!"* whenever someone does something that we consider uniquely Black and a private (in house) act.

Black men who fought in any war for this country would return home and they would never receive the same heroes welcome as their white counterparts. Between the end of Reconstruction and the years following World War

II, there were thousands of Black veterans who were attacked, assaulted, accosted and many were lynched (Equal Justice Institute 2017). Our appearance was never the issue and we must stop lying to ourselves. It is actually the idea according to racists that Black people are naturally and permanently inferior (Equal Justice Institute, 2017). There existed a dream for many African Americans that donning the *uniform* would earn them respect and human dignity and this perspective almost always resulted in disappointment (Equal Justice Institute, 2017). What this time period further proved is that regardless of how you showed up or how respectable you presented as, white supremacy did not care. It still does not care. This social commitment to some level of racial uplift often politically links representational justice and Black America's control of their respectable image to cultural visibility as routes to racial improvement (Gray 2016). The constant disputes over respectability are often waged explicitly over "bad objects" or behaviors, practices, and expressions that are not heteronormative (Gray 2016). What we often see in Black religiosity is the reinforcing of heteronormativity as a God ordained principle without exception or you are damned to hell. What Black millennials wrestle with is the concept of God loving all of his children even the raping, pillaging, racists but the queer people is where the line is drawn. *How Sway?!* Normativity is central to whiteness and white supremacy so why are we as Black people so hell bent on enforcing it?

Imani Perry (2011) schooled us on Black exceptionalism where she argues that it establishes itself as the norm and measures everything Black against it. It is why the *bourgeoisie* or the *exceptional* Black folks can thumb their nose at any person who is Black but they operate outside of Black exceptional normativity. This behavior allows for Black people to replace our white oppressors as their gatekeepers and dons of checks and balances. *The audacity!* When you are not mindful of your liberatory practices you might very easily replace the very people that you are seeking respite from as the new purveyors of oppression. The Black Church often takes on this role of Black exceptionalism and normativity along with the Black elites who police Blackness. The exceptional condition according to Gray (2016) creates normative boundaries around subjects of respectability aimed at protecting them from potential racial and class confusion. The intention is to make certain that those who are seen as "respectable" are not painted with the same broad strokes as those who are considered immoral (Gray 2016). The politics of respectability are successful in that they are aimed at providing a class distinction to members of the Black affluent classes and separating them from the non-normative practices of the less affluent Black people (Gray 2016). As times have changed and members of Black LGBTQ communities have become more visible, heteronormative disapproval of nonconforming persons and sexual practices seemed to strike a nerve with Black Church members determined to protect heteronormative definitions of Black man and woman-hood and the definition of family (Gray 2016). *Who are you to determine how someone else identifies with a man made social construct like gender?* How we choose to manage boundaries as well as our moral judgement which is used to regulate sociocultural, social, and sexual practices most certainly plays a role in the subjection to the discourse of respectability politics and fighting for liberation (Gray 2016). Black religiosity often takes a chapter directly out of the playbook of white evangelicalism and that is never a good thing.

WHITE RELIGIOSITY (EVANGELICALISM)

White people and their religion are truly American concepts. Wars have been fought over the ability to worship how they see fit, and to worship whom they please. However, this does not by default prepare white people to be tolerant of the religious practices and experiences of others. Whiteness and white religiosity is the forced standard version that all persons living in this social experiment or *New World* were expected to follow. White people were so serious about their religion that they indoctrinated those indigenous to America and the enslaved Africans that they stole during the antebellum era. White people and evangelicalism in America is a truly terrifying concept because they [white people] use it to justify and rationalize their behaviors. If any other non-white ethnic group clung to their religion and acted out certain behaviors as a result of their religion, they would be labeled extremists. White people consistently act out as a result of evangelicalism, and everyone pretends not to notice.

For a brief period of time between the civil rights movements and the election of President Barack Obama white people pretended to be disgusted by racism. This false narrative is what made people believe that we had arrived in a time of being *post-racial* and that being *colorblind* was a good thing to say about yourself. What we would learn in 2016 is that those people were simply awaiting their turn. The election of Donald J. Trump, coupled with the rise of right-wing religious popularity, caused there to be a referendum on anything equitable or anti-racist (Kivisto 2019). White people and their relationship to religious extremism is a central tenet of white supremacy. The Protestant Reformation served as the impetus to the rise of European expansion and capitalism (Comer 1969). The movement towards uncontrolled greed accompanied with a sense of entitlement is what led us to where we are today. Racism in America according to Comer (1969), grows out of the social conditions of the 16th century Europe and Africa and was then shaped by forces specific to the formation, political ferment, religiosity, geography, and economics of what would become the United States. The racism enacted by white people is a low-level defense and adjustment mechanism utilized to deal with their own psychological and social insecurities as explained by Comer (1969).

This perspective allows you to understand that racism and white supremacy are sparred from white male inadequacy and the belief that they are simply not enough. It is inherently why white male mediocrity is celebrated as the standard and when anyone bests white people, they are labeled a cheater, questioned, and often villainized. Racism in a racist society is transmitted from generation to generation as a positive social value similar to patriotism, good manners, and religiosity (Comer 1969). Religious anecdotes and indoctrination have always been used to pacify whiteness and rationalize their violence as God's will. Whiteness for most white people is a source of personal and social value and pride (Reyna, Bellovary, and Harris 2022). As I previously mentioned, whiteness as an ideology instills proponents of entitlement via the deserving of special treatment, rights, and privileges (Reyna et al. 2022). The coupling of this sense of superiority, moral rightness, and deserving spirit, all affixed to a religious practice creates the extremism. America is also changing and that poses a threat to white religious extremists' vision of the country. What I always find interesting is that European Americans, who themselves are immigrants, would have such an audacious dislike for a shifting racial demographic. Particularly considering that they were the initial people who forced America to change from a nation of non-white people to one where white people are the ruling class. How do you enter someone else's home as a guest and then become violent at the thought of other house guests? That my friend, is the ridiculousness of whiteness and racism. White religious extremists are also the purveyors of mass genocide in America.

Every other ethnic group in America has had to face off against white supremacy at some point in history and yet white people are the people most concerned with being systematically wiped out. The "theory" of white genocide suggests that a combination of lower white birthrates, the decline of the family structure, access to abortions, and immigration from non-European countries is accelerating their erasure (Reyna et al. 2022). I remember being in conversation a few years back with an administrative assistant at a former institution and her telling me very flatly, *"We vote red no matter what!"* and one could assume her perspectives on most other issues although she appeared to be what Professor Jesse Daniels would refer to as a *nice white lady.* The idea of *blind patriotism* or unquestioning support for the U.S. even if/when it is complicit in injustice, wrongdoing, or even mass atrocities (Perry and Schleifer 2022) is white supremacy. White people [Americans] who conflate Christian and American identities are most likely to sacralize "the nation" to the extent of whitewashing its past and endorsing it without question (Perry and Schleifer 2022). To be clear, American-ness is an implication of white-ness and your willingness to assimilate into it (Perry and Schleifer 2022). Which then allows for "Christian America" to bolster faux perceptions of white Americans being chosen, fundamentally good, and morally righteous (Perry and Schleifer 2022). As stated by Perry & Schleifer (2022), among the most salient historical challenges to America's "goodness" as a nation, and also consequently the axis for both justified contention and disagreement, revolves around its racial history.

Pretending that racism and white supremacy are not central to the framing and development of the United States is unforgivably dense. Another close connection to the whitewashing patriarchal patriotic project that is America, is the belief that it is a Christian nation, founded on biblical principals and good values (Perry and Schleifer 2022). America is no more righteous than it is racist and that is putting it mildly. White people often deny the centrality of racism in America's history, while African Americans, Native Americans, Hispanic Americans, and Asian Americans are forced to be cognizant of its legacies while living with white supremacy as a norm (Perry and Schleifer 2022). What is key to remember is that not even white people are safe from white supremacy and white religious extremism. White Americans tend to often rationalize bad religious actors as one-offs even though the data exists to support that it is more than a singular bad actor in most instances of extremism. This is not surprising since they often do the same when it per-tains to identifying racist people in their own families. White people at large tend not to care about issues that impact other people and will rationalize it as something that the person or people did to be deserving of particular cir-cumstances. It poses an interesting dichotomy for people who profess to be the most religious among us to be known as the people who care-less about anyone not racialized as white. *Or at least it should!*

The diabolical way that racism is interwoven into white religiosity is the same way that it exists in the world. There are no explicit references to racial or ethnic identity (Perry and Schleifer 2022) when reviewing religious doctrine and policies. However, white religious extremism is very similar to policies created by institutions of learning at all levels where they attempt to be race neutral while directly attacking and targeting marginalized groups. Although extremists of all political and religious stripes proclaim to want to right great wrongs; to represent that which is self-sacrificing and noble; and to lead the wayward back to times of old or to a new beginning (Adolph 2021), they are all terribly incorrect. They tend to be utterly convinced of the rectitude of their "cause" which makes them self-righteous and outright extravagant in their assertions (Adolph 2021). If you have been listening to the far right over the past few years they are nearly robotic in their stances, arguing that abortion is wrong regardless of rape, incest, or well-being of the mother. The idea that rape and incest are not reasoning enough to allow for a mother to seek abortion if she so chooses is absolute and utter misogyny. These beliefs are no different than enslavers who raped enslaved African women for the purpose of producing more "property." It is completely archaic and maddening that any person believes the former to be acceptable, regardless of your stance on religion. The issue for me is that many of these individuals are the same folks who call themselves "allies" and that is the most perplexing part. My former admin was one of the sweetest white women I have ever worked with, but the fact that she consistently votes against my best interests means that she is inherently and firmly invested in white supremacy. You cannot be okay with any element of white supremacy and consider yourself a good or morally sound person, the math just does not math that way.

BEYOND ALLYSHIP

At my current institution I sat in a full day DEI retreat recently and there were multiple things about the day that rang performative and did not sit well with me. One of the things that rang the loudest for me was when the presenter made a snide remark about her being an ally and although updated terms exist, she prefers keeping with the "old" term. She scoffed at the words "accomplice" and "co-conspirator" which are the terms that more critical scholars are using to properly name the role that anti-racist white people play in the fight for liberation. One of the things that stuck out for me was how she made sure that her identities were stated [queer and a woman] while making light of more preferred and updated terms. It was those comments among a few other flagrant terms that were used that confirms why someone having a terminal degree and marginalized identities does not automatically equip them to be an expert or facilitator on DEI efforts. Anti-Black racism must be understood as a cornerstone of your work, and it cannot be an afterthought to your own marginalized identities. Whiteness is situated in diversity work and the purpose of disrupting the status-quo is to disrupt the appearance and centering of it, not to make additional room for it. As we look at organizations, academic institutions, and white people who don the ally flag there are often times striking similarities to racists.

For starters, many of them refuse to openly discuss and disown white supremacy. They also never openly discuss their journey of being a person born with systemic privileges and how they moved toward anti-racism. They often present as a person who has always been on the side of right and that is a peculiar position to take. A white person in America who considers themselves to be one of the most radical liberals to ever exist, they must still do battle with their relationship with white supremacy. If they have never confronted their relationship and their families' relationship with white supremacy, they cannot be a true co-conspirator or accomplice.

White supremacy jumps out at some of the most inopportune times. It could happen during the course of a conversation or during a random interaction with a marginalized person. It is not always physically violent, and it can most assuredly be an assumption that is rooted in a deep-seated stereotype that one might possess. Regardless how good of a white person you believe yourself to be, you must come face to face with the atrocities of your history in the social experiment that is America. You have to confront how you see yourself in the scope of the American story, patriotism, and white supremacy pre and post your racial awakening. That story must be told as you attempt to stand in the space and fight for liberation, lead DEI trainings, publish scholarly work, and train future leaders of tomorrow. Burying parts of your identity that were shameful, harmful, or indoctrinated and not publicly owning that is an affront to being a critical scholar of race, liberatory work, and allyship. *Who are you? Who were you? And how did you arrive at this moment in time?* Each of these are questions that you must sit with and critically analyze before you, a privileged person, seek to take part in or facilitate any attempts at racial reconciliation, liberation, or disruptive work. Who you are and what you are about must be clear so that it cannot become a distraction or a war raging internally because you refuse to deal with your truth.

Allyship simply does not do enough because it allows the people not fully invested in liberatory work to hide amongst us. Being a co-conspirator requires that you stand up and be unrelenting in your anti-racism, commit to listening and understanding, and able to pass the torch for others to lead (Ekpe and Toutant 2022). Whiteness is still allowed space within the confines of allyship because it does not readily ask that you fully give up your relationship to white supremacy, it only asks that you be nice to "certain" people in groups that you prefer. Being a co-conspirator is akin to have the conscious voice that resides within all of us that calls you in even when no one else is watching. The voice that forces you to directly address the parts of you that still align with white supremacy and forces you to purge yourself of them. It is not comfortable nor is it cute and it absolutely should not be. Many colleges and university presidents often struggle with condemning ant-Black racism when they issue campus wide statements (Ekpe and Toutant 2022), which is indicative of how the country views this targeted hate. The same institutions who refuse to condemn anti-Black racism are also the same spaces that host the absolute most DEI trainings and consider themselves to be anti-racist. *How?!* Anti-Black racism is one of the only forms of hate where people can play directly in our faces and if we react, we are considered out of line. To be anti-racist and to be a co-conspirator means that you are fully and wholly intentional about your role in and support of the liberation of the oppressed.

Allyship does not have a direct relationship with anti-racism and thereby does not hold to account its membership. In short, it does not go far enough in its efforts to be liberatory and is a bit shortsighted for not doing so. The early works of allyship most notably assisted persons of non-marginalized identities with being active participants in supporting the LGBTQ+ community.

However, as is common within the LGBTQ+ community, anti-Black racism is not always presumed to be included in their work and only recently have there been efforts to include Black cis and trans persons. Anti-racist, co-conspirator, and liberatory frameworks all work in tandem to emphasize and overemphasize the importance of acknowledging and admonishing anti-Black racism as key to disrupting white supremacy and racism in all of its forms. As stated by Ekpe & Toutant (2022), times are changing and times have changed, and how we make sense of and conceptualize allyship must involve critical critique, action, and intentionality in reimagining a means to do true liberatory work. That work must always include anti-racist, activist, and co-conspirator work in order to have true merit and teeth. The merit and teeth are something that are almost always missing from most institutional DEI initiatives that do not expressly name the oppressor, and why disruption is a public good. Allyship has always been situated within the context of being "safe" and less risky. It does not call for those who protest to be upholders of it to take personal risks by endangering their livelihoods, comfort, physical being, and in certain situations their freedom (Ekpe and Toutant 2022). Allyship is the pumpkin spice version of activism.

In addition to participating in an internal inquiry it is of the utmost importance that white co-conspirators never lean into white saviordom. White people tend to believe that marginalized people cannot help themselves and that somehow their marginalized experience is somehow related to some deficit that they genetically possess. This shows up in many industries, but it is especially present in the education discipline at the primary, secondary, and tertiary educational levels. White saviordom is a concept that helps make sense of how white people often center themselves as exceptional and necessary to the betterment of a marginalized group through liberalism. Well-intentioned white people often slip into paternalism when they believe they are protecting or supporting people of color (Ekpe and Toutant 2022). The belief that white people are ultimately superior is reflected in how they show up to assist and it is necessary that the self-work is authentic, consistent, and ongoing or white supremacy as I mentioned before will most assuredly emerge. As a result, allyship and saviordom reside on the same side of the coin and no one needs that "version" of liberal activism.

Deficit based ideologies about what the marginalized need are ever-present among liberal educators who perceive themselves to be anti-racist. Interventions led by white people have often been central to educational policy and it is extremely prominent in the context of neoliberal reform (Sondel, Kretchman and Dunn 2022). As indicated by Sondel et al. (2022), white supremacy is not solely the extreme political movement of the bold and hateful racists, but it is also the everyday white perspectives that are centered and are protective of white interests. Most of which are held staunchly by people who like to remind us of their Black friends, partners, lovers, or baby-sitters. They fail to realize that when they describe their relationships with Black people, they always mention the Black folks in some sort of service to them. A huge red flag! Please stop telling us this, I can assure you that we do not care. White people often believe that these stories certify and cement how "down" they are with Black people and the cause. All it does for me is certify and cement how unaware they actually are and how dangerous it is that they consider that ideology both liberal and anti-racist, let alone allyship. Your resistance cannot be on the back of Blackness or Black people. Sleeping with a Black man to spite your dad is not the move that you believe it is. In fact, it only further cements that you do not realize your role in white supremacy and your subsequent fetishization of Black people.

Understanding whiteness is key to the understanding of white supremacy itself, as well as how to dismantle and disrupt the aforementioned system (Sondel et al. 2022). In order to be a true co-conspirator and anti-racist you must constantly be in critique of whiteness as a norm in need of disruption not saving or exception. In order to properly prepare, white co-conspirators must understand that their assistance in liberation is in concert with the marginalized and they must never position themselves as the most necessary aspects for change to occur (Stanley and Schroeder 2022). Another aspect that must be directly addressed in preparation for moving toward a co-conspirator framework is that white people and their ability to play obtuse as it pertains to issues surrounding race and racism systemically and as it occurs in real-time. There often exists an "unknowing" that white persons exhibit as it pertains to the discussion of race, perhaps more of a willful ignorance as stated by Dempsey (2022). It allows white people to resist seeing how deeply whiteness is embedded in educational spaces and society at large (Dempsey 2022). This unknowing allows the dominant group [*white people*] to dismiss or disbelieve what Black people and other persons of color are communicating (Dempsey 2022). The work of a true collaborative liberatory movement begins with "knowing" and being intentional in the disruption of the self in conjunction with white supremacy, and then the system at large.

Operating in the obtuse as a rationale for your inaction is as problematic as your full-on participation. What we understand about the need for disruption of the status-quo is that it will require full participation of everyone claiming to be opposed to it. There can be no participants of disruption standing on the sideline and waiting to stake their claim in the "new." You have to choose the side of the marginalized and use every point of power available to you in furthering the resistance and solidifying it. The election cycles post-2020 have shown proof that the great majority of the "allies" who surfaced were not truly down for the cause. The midterms of 2022 also provided a stark contrast regarding who is fighting for liberation and who are the constant purveyors of white supremacy. Scholars, scholar-practitioners, and DEI practitioners are always tasked with being gentle as it pertains to the discussion of white supremacy and white accountability. We were chided for our abolitionists stances on why the police should absolutely be defunded. There were constant reminders that the country is politically moderate, and that progressivism was too extreme of a stance to take. What we all learned is that each and every person who uttered those words were employees of white supremacy. They were using the divide and conquer strategy to confuse and displace our progress.

Critical race theory (CRT) was never the issue since we do not teach critical theory to children. The issue was always the same as it was during colonial antebellum America and that concern was the non-elite whites joining together with Black people and people of color to overthrow whiteness and white supremacy. This is the single most reason that white parents were raiding school board meetings, banning books, and calling for the suspension or termination of anyone who they believed to be in opposition of whiteness. They were scared that the children and younger voters would realize that the social experiment that is America which relies on inequality and class distinctions to keep whiteness in power, would question it. The reality is that most white people and anti-Black non-white persons do not actually know why they hate African Americans. Most of them have never stopped to interrogate for themselves why this system that they so staunchly protect should still exist. The lines have been drawn and the sides are clear. You are either anti-racist or racist and you are either anti-fascist or fascist, there is no middle. My challenge to you is for you to begin questioning why you are still participating in white supremacy and most importantly when do you plan to stop?

REFERENCES

Adolph, Robert Bruce. 2021. "American Extremism: The far right of the US Republican Party." *Atlantisch Perspectief Vol. 45 No.3* 25–29.

Barnes, Sandra L. 2006. "An Analysis of Black Church Usage of Black Liberation and Womanist Theologies: Implications and Inclusivity." *Race, Gender & Class Vol. 13 Number 3–4* 329–346.

Blakemore, Erin. 2019. *Why America's First Colonial Rebels Burned Jamestown to the Ground: Bacon's Rebellion was triggered when a grab for Native lands was denied.* August 2. https://www.history.com/news/bacons-rebellion-jamestown-colonial-america.

Collins, Sam P.K. 2018. *Millennials Breaking from Organized Religion.* September 5. https://www.washingtoninformer.com/millennials-breaking-from-organized-religion/.

Comer, James P. Dec. 1969. "White Racism: Its Root, Form, and Function." *American Journal of Psychiatry Vol. 126 Issue 6* 777–916.

Dempsey, Anne. 2022. "Decentering Whiteness in the Social Work Classroom." *Journal of Teaching in Social Work 42:2–3* 175–189.

Ekpe, Leslie, and Sarah Toutant. 2022. "Moving Beyond Performative Allyship: A Conceptual Framework for Anti-Racist Co-conspirators." In *Developing Anti-Racist Practices in the Helping Professions: Inclusive Theory, Pedagogy, and Application*, by Kaprea Johnson, Narketta Sparkman-Key, Alan Meca and Shauntay Tarver, 67–92. Cham: Palgrave MacMillan.

Gray, Herman. 2016. "Introduction: Subject to Respectability." *Souls: A Critical Journal of Black Politics, Culture, and Society Vol 18:2–4* 192–200.

Harris, Paisely Jane. 2003. "Gatekeeping and Remaking: The Politics of Respectability in African American Women's History and Black Feminism." *Journal of Women's History Volume 15 Number 1* 212–220.

Institute, Equal Justice. 2017. *Lynching in America: Targeting Black Veterans.* Montgomery: Equal Justice Institute.

Kivisto, Peter. 2019. "The Politics of Cruelty." *The Sociological Quarterly Vol. 60 No.2* 191–200.

Kohli, R, M Pizarro, and A Nevárez. 2017. "The 'New Racism' of K–12 Schools: Centering Critical Research on Racism." *Review of Research in Education* 182–202.

Love, Bettina. 2020. *Education Week.* June 12. Accessed September 17, 2022. https://www.edweek.org/leadership/opinion-an-essay-for-teachers-who-understand-racism-is-real/2020/06.

Perry, Imani. 2011. *More Beautiful and More Terrible.* New York: New York University Press.

Perry, Samuel, and Cyrus Schleifer. 2022. "My country, white or wrong: Christian nationalism, race, and blind patriotism." *Ethnic and Racial Studies* 1–20.

Project, Black Youth. 2019. *Millennials aren't skipping church, the Black Church is skipping us.* December 31. http://blackyouthproject.com/millennials-arent-skipping-church-the-black-church-is-skipping-us/.

Reyna, Christina, Andrea Bellovary, and Kara Harris. 2022. "The Psychology of White Nationalism: Ambivalence Toward a Changing America." *Social Issues and Policy Review Vol. 16 No.1* 79–124.

Sondel, Beth, Kerry Kretchman, and Alyssa Hadley Dunn. 2022. "'Who Do These People Want Teaching Their Children?' White Saviorism, Colorblind Racism, and

Anti-Blackness in 'No Excuses' Charter Schools." *Urban Education Volume 57 Issue 9* 1621–1650.

Stanley, Melissa, and Stephanie Schroeder. 2022. "Problematizing White Allyship in the Civil Rights Curriculum of Studies Weekly." *The Social Studies* 1–18.

Chapter 2

By Any Mean's Necessary

Discovery of the Self and One's Own Blackness

DISCOVERY OF THE SELF

Nina Simone was insistent about making sure that we knew that Black power, Blackness, and our culture would make Black folks more curious about who we are. She believed that if she used her voice to create a curiosity about who we are and how we have been kept away from who we really are we would become curious about finding ourselves. In order for Blackness to be liberated those who hold genetic stock in her must be brought to bear. Many of us have not yet realized the royalty that exists within us, and how that unwavering reality causes our oppressors to constantly react with malicious intent. Their rage is because they see who we are and what we are capable of. However, it is due to centuries of subjugation that many of us have allowed our light to dwindle. We allow our light to dwindle because of fear of what allowing our fullness to shine could mean. Calling each of us into ourselves and into who we are will allow us to recognize our role in our liberation. For many African Americans, there is a constant battle between what we want to do and what we should do. This battle is largely because we are not allowed to just be, and we are often forced into a place of surviving. What a difference this world would look like if Blackness were allowed to thrive without restriction. The restriction of Blackness has been the intention and contributor of the success of white supremacy.

European colonizers who kidnapped our people were always terrified of the day that we would realize our collective power. One of the most successful attributes of white supremacy is its unique power to be able to create division through the *divide-and-conquer* strategy. We spend so much of our time competing for our time in the sun of oppression that we spend zero time fighting for our collective liberation. The success of white supremacy is that it keeps the marginalized and the minoritized warring against each other and competing for gold in the oppression Olympics.

Making sure that no one forgets that you are the most oppressed among your group members is a waste of time, effort, and energy. Your focus should be situated in the understanding of who you and your people are. Another true success of white supremacy is how it has caused us to deny Africa as our motherland while trying to convince ourselves that we value our Blackness. I remember growing up and often hearing people refute any relation or relationship to Africa yet proudly proclaiming to be Black. We know where Africa is situated geographically and that most of us derive from the western portion of the continent. What I am curious to know is where exactly on the world map is *Black* located? Historically, we were labeled as Black by white people as an attempt to other our existence and to keep us at odds about our identity, value, and relationship to Africa. I am quick to make it plain for folks and I will assist you in your learning as well. *Listen closely!* My culture is Black because my people reimagined a word intended to strip us of our dignity and humanity. My nationality is American by force but not by grace or choice. Lastly, I am African by ethnicity and ancestral lineage, and I am damn proud of it! Black is culture and Black is indeed beautiful but be clear that it is no replacement for what was stolen from us—*Africa!*

Understanding your Blackness and your relationship to it must be as intentional as your work in divorcing yourself from white supremacy and its core tenets: anti-Blackness, homophobia, transphobia, colorism, anti-poverty, fatphobia, xenophobia, religiosity, the carceral state, and patriarchy. Understand that each of these things were created to disallow for us to see the humanity of the marginalized and to feel that we are somehow above them because we either avoided or survived any of the aforementioned core tenets. White supremacy is funny because it has so many of us confident about being better than our *sistas* and *brothas* in the Black struggle. One of the more intentional things I always try to impart upon my students as a source of wisdom and saving grace is that our work, our very intentional work, must be liberatory for the most marginalized among us. Many of us believe that our measurement of success is how something directly or indirectly impacts us. A measurement of success should always be asking *"how might this benefit or impress Black folks who are more marginalized than me?"*

MY BLACKNESS, YOUR BLACKNESS, OUR BLACKNESS!

The journey of one-thousand understandings must begin with you. For hundreds of years the structurally and systemically oppressed and their descendants have had a love/hate relationship with their conditions and most importantly with their Blackness. Our struggle with understanding the power and might of our collective Blackness is that it is constantly marred by struggle. The struggle for far too often has taken center stage and disallows for us to be able to view its beauty because its pain is always so much more evident. As Cross (1981) tell us, Black people go through stages of understanding in relation to their self-identity or Black identity. It is often important to note that there is a direct connection between how Black people view themselves and how Blackness as a concept is either valued or devalued in their upbringing (Cross 1981). The intent is not to place the lack of belonging or responsibility in destabilizing anti-Black racism on Black parents or Black families, but it is intended to highlight that positive reinforcements tend to make a difference.

As a child I can recall my own mistreatment because of my complexion in comparison to my own siblings. The mistreatment never happened in our home via my parents, but it did happen when we were with people entrusted with our care. There were two young Black women in particular who my mom trusted to watch over us and it was through the two of them that I was taught to devalue my own complexion and subsequently my own Blackness. My brother, sister, and I are what we refer to as "stairsteps" which essentially means that we are all close in age and our heights were like stairsteps and believe it or not they still are. That piece is important to understand why they were also too young to protect me from what was happening to me. I am the middle child, my brother is a year older, and my sister is just under two years younger than I. We were approximately five, four, and two years of age when these incidents occurred. Very rarely did the two young women babysit us together but there might have been a time or two when the dual babysitting did occur. One of them pulled black pieces of rubber off of the doormat and would throw them at me, and the other would not allow me to eat lunch at the table with my siblings because I was apparently too dark. I was forced to sit on the floor to eat my food as my siblings sat together at the table eating theirs. I would eventually tell my mother about the abuse years later and I believe I asked her not to make a big deal of it. One of the women died of cancer prematurely in her late 20s and the other has since raised her own children. The scars of that experience are still with me, and I am full of emotion as I write this out for the first time. I, like so many other

Black children did not deserve that abuse. What resonates more for me now is that the young women who decided to harm me were obviously carrying their own harm regarding complexion and Blackness as a result of white supremacy. I forgive them.

Our relationship to our identity is ever-changing and vast because through reading and education you will begin to see your own ignorance fade and your enlightenment emerge. It is how I have been able to make sense of what happened to me and understand why someone might find complexion as a thing worthy of violence. If we pay attention to the way that complexions are discussed, who among women is considered beautiful or "exotic look-ing," and who is considered more masculine and less attractive it all stems from our devaluing of all shades of Blackness and our relationship to white supremacy. How we take part in or appear in relationship to our Blackness is directly linked to how we were brought into contact with it. For many, Black love, Black power, and Black value was essential to their upbringing and positionality. For others, the acknowledgment of Blackness with intention was always secondary to being. An assumption of sorts that many believe will come to fruition on its own or when an individual is ready or inquisitive. I can say with all certainty that this is a terrible idea and a rather problematic approach. Consider how children, teens, and young adults learn about sex when their parents were too scared to talk to them about it. Race, culture, and identity are key to understanding who you are in a world that hates you sim-ply because you exist. Why would we leave that teaching up to the universe? The intentionality of your self-discovery is as essential to your development as finding out what cologne or perfume scents work best for you.

George Jerry Sefa Dei (2017) states, that he engages his Black and African identity as a space and site of experiential knowing. He further states that he is intentional about putting forth a particular interest to reinvent an *Africanness* in *Diasporic* contexts where being Black and being African mat-ter in profound ways (Dei 2017). To understand how we might reimagine an existence where we know from conception that our Black is indeed beautiful, royal, intentional, and divine starts with instilling it within our daily Black beings and doings. We cannot allow whiteness and white contexts to be our introduction to being Black in the American racialized hierarchical context. Doing so most assuredly guarantees that the version taught to you is one that centers whiteness as the standard and Blackness as the curse. I have had dis-cussions with millennial Black parents who feel that they want to keep anti-Black racism from their children as long as possible and for them to grow up in their innocence as long as possible.

Unfortunately, America does not allow us the liberty of such a freedom. Not preparing your babies for the reality of who they are and how they show up in the world is like playing a deadly game of Russian roulette. Dei (2017) further states, as people who ascend and descend from Africa, we deny our Black identity and our own constructed Blackness at our peril. When we fail to lay claim to who we are and grow with that knowledge we open ourselves up to violence within and external to our existence. *Name and claim!* If we understand that anti-Blackness has stood as the dominant societal logic and is responsible for shaping the configuration and character of American social institutions (Jenkins 2021), why would we assume that we do not need to be intentional about heading off anti-Blackness before it takes hold? Most of our negative self-assessments occurred once we left the safety of our parents and attended school. It is then where parts of who you are began to be inter-rogated and picked apart by peers and even the adults who are tasked with teaching and protecting you. A self-assured Black child who has been primed and prepared their entire life for how to exist on their own terms and in lock-and-step with their ancestors is a child ready to rise above any bouts of internalized anti-Blackness. What my own abuse did to me was that it caused me to question everything about my features and why I looked the way that I did. I compared the features of my siblings to my own and wondered why there were differences. My mother certainly loved on us, as did our extended family, and one of my great aunties said that my dimples meant that I had been kissed by angels. None of that mattered because all of it was surface and none of it did the work of showing us how to understand our Blackness.

There is no fault to be placed on how our parents raised us and how my mother as the primary parent loved on us. They were young and even in their teaching us about our history, the in-depth dialogue of what Blackness is, and how we were uniquely situated in it, that talk never occurred. It is likely because they did not know how to have the conversation. As an expert and critical scholar, I find myself educating them both on the subject of Blackness, anti-Blackness, and white supremacy in ways that I know they have never taught me. Essentially, they were not equipped for the in-depth dialogue and to be quite honest many of our parents are not. Unless you grew up in a home full of Black folks who were rooted in their identity and what that means as a descendant of the formerly enslaved, you also were underpre-pared for how to battle anti-Blackness within. It is in my most gracious and yet honest assessment that most people have no idea of what white supremacy actually is. Yes, we all know about the very obvious acts and implications of it. However, most people do not understand that white supremacy is sealed into the cracks of the buildings that we live in and grown into the foods that we consume. It is quite literally and immeasurably, everywhere!

OUR INHERITANCE UPSETS THE OPPRESSOR

When I speak of our inheritance I am not necessarily speaking about money or things of earthly value. I am speaking solely of our ancestral inheritance; who we come from; and how they live-on within us. The goal of enslavement and the creation of race was to create a racialized hierarchy that allowed for whiteness to remain a ruling class and for the enslaved and their descendants to forever remain subservient to whiteness. Our ancestors were not docile people nor were they simply going along to get along. Within their struggle also brewed their resistance and their unsinkable joy. That is the inheritance that we [the descendants] received. Many of us spend so much time chasing things and desiring to be accepted by or in proximity to whiteness. While on and moving through the journey of white acceptance many of us move further away from Black understanding along with connection and kinship. This is evident by the way anti-Blackness appears within and resonates so deeply with so many of us. I have certainly witnessed enough of our people caping for whiteness, and I am always confused like, are you deadass right now? I often want to grab hold of my people and shake them free from themselves. I deeply wish for all of us to realize who we are; who we have been made to be; and who we actually come from, so we can make peace with it. The shame was never in our enslavement. The shame resides with those who saw fit to enslave us.

Our progression and survival hinges upon us realizing who we actually are and that there is nothing wrong with us. As part of your awakening and coming into yourself you must first accept that we are a formidable people and that has always scared white people. Whiteness has always forced us to play small and through tactics of mind manipulation it makes you believe that in order to make white people safe that you must diminish yourself. I recall a time when I worked on a graduate admissions team where there were only two Black men. Myself, and my colleague who I will refer to as Ronnie were the two Black men on the team. There were other Black men that worked for the organization, but we were certainly not heavy in numbers. Ronnie was often called upon by our white colleagues to "rap." Ronnie had previously shared with the team that he had a musical talent. This disclosure occurred long before I joined the team, so I was never quite certain what prompted it. What I do recall is the periodic requests of Ronnie to perform a rap during team lunches and gatherings. I was always confused and slightly agitated when he would burst into song on demand. It often made me wonder if this was Ronnie's way of making everyone feel that he was not dangerous or if it was something else. Ronnie like everyone else on the team was college educated and credentialed so I never quite understood his burden. What I do know is that his burden is not unique, and it is one that so many Black folks carry. The burden where the safety of all white folks present is somehow your responsibility. I am also a person who is musically gifted, but I would be damned if I ever volunteered to perform for whiteness. There is a unique difference in performing for the joy of your soul juxtaposed to performing for your oppressor because they demanded it. I have always rejected the performance of safety because white people have never once performed it for me. The idea that a people who have the ability to end your life at a moments notice need you to "perform" to make them feel at ease has always rattled my spirit.

If you think back through your own life and some of the decisions that you have made. Ask yourself if you ever gave-in to the performance. Then ask yourself why you did it. There is something that through the DNA shared with our enslaved ancestors that makes some of us feel that this performance is necessary. We feel that it is so necessary that when others of us decide not to participate in the performance that we might look at them funny. In that exact moment you need to name it. Name the moment where you decided that the performance is essential and that anyone who decides not to per-form is an affront to respectable Blackness. As I think of the performance of respectability and who gets to decide when that performance must occur, I am reminded of the Oscars in 2022 and *the slap*. There was an immediate distancing of those who still see no problem with the performance of respect-able negrodom *in spite of*, and the one who violated the unspoken agreement we share with white folks. One of his most ardent dissenters on the morning that followed was a Black male morning TV anchor who until that moment I greatly admired and respected. The TV anchor went on and on about how *the slap* took us as Black people backwards, I felt no such way. He and many others helped to craft this narrative that the Black actor who broke the agree-ment must surrender himself to the will of white people and second-hand Black embarrassment. Eight months later that same morning TV anchor who ranted about how embarrassing and defaming to Black people the slap was, was outed for having an affair with his white woman co-anchor.

One of the things that remains true is that anti-Blackness has no race, reli-gion, or geographic location that confines it. The one quality that anti-Black-ness has that is resounding among all of its purveyors is audacity. Most of us do not care what two consenting adults do in their personal time but it was the audacity that was and is often present that boggles me. Defending your Black wife from personal attacks is a horrendous endeavor but cheating on your Black wife with your married white colleague is not? Part of being aware of how you perform for whiteness is being mindful of how you criticize Black folks who through recognition of their power will not. Black people who are walking in their inheritance and being unashamed to disappoint white people underscores the need for liberation. White people and their perceptions of us cannot be how we measure what is or is not appropriate. Personally, I would never disown or scowl at a Black man for honorably protecting his Black wife and family regardless of the location. Black women and Black people are deserving of that level of unashamed protection, period. The performance of respectability is one that Black people must absolutely disassociate from.

Knowing who you are is key to understanding how to harvest and cultivate your inheritance and your power. Your understanding of who actually holds the power is part of your work. White people recognize and know it and they always have. It is expressly why white people at every opportunity they receive will attempt to strike it down. As long as whiteness has us questioning or justifying who we are and to whom we belong it will keep us distracted from walking in our abundance. I remember in my younger years people would often make fun of the Black folks who seemed to understand it.

The pan-Africanists; the people who wore locs and natural hair before they were fashionable; and the folks who said only we could save us, they were often mocked. I did not have the language or knowledge to understand it at all but after reflecting on it I know that the responses toward those individuals was rooted in anti-Blackness. I am often brought to this point of reflection when we discuss spaces for higher education and their suitability. There exists this dynamic that anything remotely situated in Blackness is not inherently good enough. We see this discourse often situated around HBCUs and their affordability; ability to prepare Black students for the real world; and their facilities and upkeep. The conversation happens so much that Black folks and white folks who did not attend HBCUs join together in their negative critiques of HBCU spaces. My entire higher education career which stems from enrollment management to student affairs and the academy have all been situated at PWIs. These experiences have allowed me to be a spectator in a space my people were not initially intended to be in. What I can certainly say is that the same issues that HBCUs face regarding facilities, affordability, and real-world preparation of Black students also exist at PWIs.

PWIs do not garner the same negative critiques from Black or white people because they have convinced themselves that they are inherently better, in spite of. People have also not asked the question about why HBCUs are so underfunded and under-resourced and why these are indeed acts of state sanctioned white supremacy. When I last worked in enrollment management, I was responsible for facilitating, curating, and overseeing a graduate feeder pipeline between Florida Agricultural and Mechanical University (FAMU) and American University where I was employed. One of the things that I learned during that time was how racism in Florida and in particularly in Tallahassee is the reason why FAMUs law school is in Orlando and Florida States' law school is in Tallahassee even though FAMU had a law school in Tallahassee, first. The same attack of white supremacy is why FAMUs hospital which was the only hospital to treat African Americans in North Florida was also closed. FAMU was attacked because there were constant questions about the need for Florida State and FAMU to exist in the same city separated only by train tracks (Hatter 2019). We all know when white people start asking questions about Black folks and Black spaces at any given time that destruction or interruption of some sort will soon follow. The State of Florida would yank FAMU's school of law funding in 1965 and transfer the funds to Florida State University (Hatter 2019). This act of white concern and aggression would cause FAMU school of law to close in 1978. FAMUs hospital was attacked and ultimately defunded three years later with its funds being transferred to Tallahassee Memorial Hospital (Hatter 2019). There are instances like this one which causes a great deal of frustration among HBCU alum when non-HBCU alum who are Black and non-Black speak against our institutions without full context of the harm caused in both the past and the present. Much like Mother Africa, whiteness, and white people always move to destabilize anything remotely centered in Black existing. It is precisely why choosing to attend an HBCU in the past and in the present are acts of resistance.

RESIST GIVING UP YOUR BLACKNESS

The greatest act of resistance is to be bold and proud of your Blackness and all that comes with it. As people begin to move up in the world one of the first things, they tend to do is separate themselves apart from the very thing that created them. In the pursuit of white acceptance some people will either disassociate from their Blackness or constantly find themselves in negative critique of it. One of the ways that I have often seen this displayed is when Black folks from the hood grow up and become police officers. The belief is often that they are working to change the system from within. However, a system that is rooted in anti-Blackness will only change, you. Quite a few people I know personally have made degrading comments about our own people from their lens as police officers and federal agents without addressing the corrupt system that traps Black folks. I recall a particular conversation around the same time frame that young Black women were disappearing globally and from in an around DC. First Lady Michelle Obama and many others launched the *Bring Back Our Girls* campaign aimed at bringing awareness to the present and time sensitive issue. Nearly 300 Black girls in Nigeria had been kidnapped by Boko Haram and the hashtag was an urgent call for assistance. Six years after the original launch activists and community leaders in DC relaunched the hashtag to bring awareness to the invisibility and neglect of missing Black girls in the district (Lindsey 2020).

One of the police officers who I attended my undergraduate HBCU with states, "why is everyone making such a big deal? Most of those girls were runaways" and his loud indignation to me read as an indictment on Black girls, women, and people. Are Black girl runaways underserving of saving? I certainly disagree with such a sentiment. Particularly when we all witnessed Gabby Petito's case reach a resolution in just four months. What the Petito case showed us is that white girls and women are always priority. Her case deserved to be solved and her family deserved to know the truth, as does the families of the missing Black girls and women. If Black people who become active members of the system no longer see the value in our people, what was the point? Some folks began to look really funny in the light. When your narratives about your own people begin to sound like white supremacist talking points you have lost your way. This is the very same ideology that is often expressed when we hear public discourse about Black institutions like HBCUs. Many of us are not honest that our deepest desire is to be accepted by whiteness so that we can abandon the oppression that comes with Blackness and Black proximity. This behavior is often displayed whenever we see the tired HBCU vs. PWI debate that pops off on social media quarterly. Like clockwork and most recently in the Deion Sanders and Jackson State to Colorado maneuver. The discussion regarding the new opportunity for Sanders went from a discussion about football and Black coaches at Power 5 institutions to deficit framed dialogue aimed at de-platforming HBCUs all while lacking necessary nuance (Black, Engram and Smith 2022). What we often witness whenever there is an issue of concern for Black folks is the automatic pile-on as if the experience itself was not harsh enough. For some reason [absolutely related to slavery], Black people in general are never allowed to come up short and or not be gracious and grateful. We are expected to be statuesque even in scenarios where a loud outburst or table flip is absolutely necessary. We are expected to always be resolute and docile in the face of racialized violence and attacks. Most folks, and sometimes even us, do not give space for Black feeling or Black possibility. We are often expected to check our feelings, our history, and our oppression at the door all the while everyone else is allowed to not only bring theirs in but to also center it. Even in this present time we are still required to act as humble and appreciative as the enslaved.

Most recently a viral tweet of a young Black man [Jerry Edmond] who was being berated at a Raiders v. Patriots NFL game came across my timeline. The great majority of Black people immediately knew what we were witnessing as the white woman and her white husband taunted the young Black man, a Patriots fan, wearing his Patriots jersey at his first ever NFL game.

Her agitating of him absolutely warranted a response from him but he like many of us did not give into the called-for response. No one in the audience stopped her or stepped in to quiet her taunting. Most people would call her actions "typical" of sports fans and within that response lies my problem. In America, racialized violence against African Americans and Black people at large is always rationalized. People seem to forget that sports fandom and white supremacy absolutely intersect and allow for very violent behaviors to exist. We see it in every sport known to man and on every continent and in every country. Knowing full well the way that racism and white supremacy are present there is still an expectation that Black people, and, in this case, Jerry always be in control of ourselves. The reason being that if we choose to respond in the way that the situation calls for it could mean instantaneous death for us. White people are fully aware of their power in the moments where our encounter with them teeters on the border of life and death and yet they persist. The NFL's response, sports outlets, some Black people, and the internet at large all began applauding his ability to be calm which immediately enraged me. He was given tickets to a Patriots game where he sat with Robert Kraft who is the owner of the New England Patriots. The Oakland Raiders have not yet announced the banning of the fan and none of the media outlets who managed to find out Jerry's name have released the name of the fan who taunted him. This act is a performative one intended to move people beyond the incident. However, I, and many others are still stuck on the experience that the young man had to endure and what many African Americans must consistently endure when white people decide to have their way. Stop applauding our ability to maintain our composure amid racism and white supremacy and address why we are still expected to do so. Address why other people including folks who consider themselves to be liberal immediately saw his calm as the point of focus, and not the chaos that was the white woman. If a Black woman and her Black husband had done that very same thing to a young white man or woman, would the response be the same? I hate that I even need to draw such an obvious comparison for the obtuse to be made aware.

Blackness is not something that we can disappear from, and it matters not how cool, calm, and collected we are. When white people decide to set their sights on and target you there are very few people who will jump in to disarm the attack. We know why Black people are at times slow to involve themselves in such a scenario that could then turn the target toward their own body. What we do not understand is why white people often see these scenarios, consider themselves anti-racist, and record the scenario instead of diffusing the scenario. Understanding the liberation of the marginalized and more particularly Africans Americans means being fully aware of what white supremacy shows up as and who considers it their responsibility to disrupt.

Are there white people who have physically used their body to diffuse situations? Yes. However, they are still few and far between and because that is what you should do as a decent human being there are no awards to be given for doing so.

In revisiting the issue surrounding perceptions of HBCUs one of the things that I find most fascinating is the opinions that our own people hold. In a recent conversation with a friend who I hold dear, we disagreed on who generally ignites these toxic discussions. One of the things that was raised that I have heard before is that HBCU grads tend to gang up on people or make people feel like outsiders. Sometimes there are accusations made about HBCU grads being elitist toward other Black folks and this is baseline projection of the *uppity-negro* trope. The idea that a Black person who does not diminish themselves toward white people or in white spaces is considered *uppity*. I chuckled to myself because our homecomings alone prove this narrative to be false. I mean, have you ever been to a Prairie View, JCSU, Howard, SpelHouse, or GHOE homecoming? It is one of the most inviting Black spaces you will ever experience. HBCU grads protect and defend our institutions because the world does not, and we as alum all know and understand their value.

For this reason, if you are ever saying anything slick out of your mouth then I am certain you invited the smoke. Black PWI grads do not have their degrees devalued on the job market, while applying to graduate school, or in public discourse but HBCU alums do. This absolutely does not discount the harm experienced by Black PWI students while at their institutions. It does not at all mean that their harm is not very real and palpable but what most fail to understand is that the same purveyors of your harm at your white school are also the purveyors of minimizing the Black college experience. That must be our focus and not continuously expending our energy on the Olympics of oppression. This is the same tactic of divide and conquer that is deployed in every single situation possible to keep the marginalized at odds and we need to understand this and focus. Our aim is liberation and uplift so regardless of where you earned your degree and what discipline you enter; your job is to turn around and brings others along. The HBCU experience that I had was unique to every student who ever entered the gates on 100 Beatties Ford Road and exited via Cricket Arena/Bojangles Coliseum or the Irwin Belk Complex. This is an experience that only we share but it mirrors the experience of almost every other HBCU grad in North Carolina and across the country.

As a result of this very beautiful experience, I am self-aware, and I know to whom I belong. In my nearly seventeen-year career in higher education I have always made it a point to take the things I learned at JCSU with me. At every institution that I have worked at I have been certain to find and create community among the people who look like me because I understand what the power of community can do for a people. This is sadly not a sentiment shared by all of us and it is just a testament of the work that we still need to do. However, I do my best to make certain that every Black person that I encounter from grounds keepers, and food service workers, to the students, faculty, and administration, that each of these stakeholders receive the same respect and acknowledgment from me. We often get so caught up in ourselves and the things that are most present and most important to us that we neglect how simple things like an acknowledgment of one another can make a difference. Particularly in spaces where we are fewer in numbers. I am often the only in spaces as a Black millennial academic hoping to see someone who looks like me and often leaving disappointed. My career has provided for me a bird's eye view into what it is like being a Black person at a PWI. Which is precisely why I could never fathom any person not valuing HBCUs and majority spaces cultivated for and by Black people. Our everyday fight with white supremacy and anti-Black racism is a constant so anytime that we are able to simply be is something that I will always support, welcome, and celebrate. I need more of my people to see the value in simply existing. Existing not in the performance of whiteness or being in service of it, just existing!

EXISTING IN SPITE OF

One of the things unique to the Black existence in America is having to explain every part of our existence. The foods we eat; the way we speak; our fashion choices; our child naming rituals and name choices; and our hairstyles, are always under critique. Simply putting it, we do not have the opportunity to exist outside of the white gaze without resistance. I would be untruthful if I said that I always knew what white supremacy and anti-Black racism were in relationship to our existence. However, I can without uncertainty say that I was born to be a disruptor and I am also certain that my family and close friends would not disagree. I can recall at certain points in my development when I realized that I was experiencing racism and I absolutely pushed back in ways that would have cost me my life in times past.

From being called the n-word in peewee baseball, to being called the n-word in 6th grade and taking my 7th grade English teacher to mediation, I resisted. Each of these were forms of resistance before I knew what such a term meant and what the importance of it was. What I did know for certain was that white people would never on this side of heaven or the other, treat me any kind of way. I have always had this very unique understanding of knowing that I was purposed for something greater and that I had to always be mindful of it. Does this knowledge mean that I was not the typical teen and doing very typical teen things? No. It just means that I knew when to say no and also when to go home. Most folks who knew me well would call me a fighter and they would be correct. I was fighting anti-Blackness and I was fighting against other people's harmful expectations of me. I fought every time I, or my siblings and cousins were violated as a kid and that does not mean that I was not nurtured and loved at home because I was. I just knew early on that I was not for the bullshyt and that I would protect those that I love from any and everyone.

One thing about me is that I never went looking for trouble, but I also did not hide from it if and when it appeared either. Part of my maturing was understanding that there were indeed different ways to resist and to push back against instances of oppression that I faced without becoming violent. That maturing does not mean that I am anti-violence it just means that before I knock you to the floor, I will have tried every other measure available to me to work with and or around you, to be clear. In America, it is typical for Black folks and more specifically the descendants of the enslaved to con- stantly turn the other cheek when it comes to addressing any harm done to us. This is not something that comes natural to us, but it is something that was also forced upon us. The *Slave Codes* and the *Black Codes* have a great deal of contemporary responsibility for African Americans within the law although they are laws of the past. What most Americans fail to realize is that America never reset itself once the legal decision to end the enslavement of Africans was cemented. Reconstruction posed this opportunity, but it fell short of any long-term racial balancing. Many of the laws that restricted the freedom and movement of the enslaved are still the laws that are used to enslave the descendants in other ways. As an example, it was customary for the enslaved to accept the beating, raping, killing, and selling of their loved ones and to simply move along. This is also displayed in who actually had the right to bare arms and who was never granted the right in the first place. Free and enslaved Black persons were never allowed to strike [hit] a white person regardless of what that white person had done to them or their loved ones. Think about what would happen if a white person called the cops after starting a fight and a Black person defended themselves today. White people are fully aware that they have a 50/50 chance of having the upper hand if cops are called to any *Black vs. white* conflict.

This advantage is passed through DNA and has existed since the period of enslavement. It must be understood that when white people cause drama and then threaten to call the cops that they are playing fully into their privilege and have completely considered the response to such a dog whistle. The "codes" are why it is still seen as an act of aggression for a Black person to be in possession of a gun even if the weapon is not discharged while a white person is not. White people are expected to have the right to bare arms which is why cops approach them differently even if they are in visible distress. Many of us are not aware that many of the laws made during enslavement were not repealed or dissolved simply because slavery met its legal end. As a result of being unaware of how the very same laws that held our ancestor's captive, we find ourselves subject to the same laws without resolve. Simply existing as an African American in this country was never a right granted to us so we have to take those liberties as often as we can. Existing in the ways that we choose is most certainly an act of resistance, but it is not resistance enough. At any point in time a white man, woman, or child can decide that it is time for you to meet your end and depending on who they are connected to or where the crime occurs, they could very well get away with it. What measure of an existence is that for a people who are allegedly free? I refuse to give white people in the past, present, or future any level of authority over my body. What say you?

Our understanding of who we are and how we exist in spite of it all is key to liberating ourselves fully. The distraction and the Olympics of oppression takes up most of our time through distraction so that many of us do not have the capacity to focus on moving toward collective liberation. If white people did not understand the power that we possess they would not spend every waking moment configuring ways to keep us fighting for resources to simply exist at the bare minimum. As long as the purveyors of oppression and racialized hierarchy can keep the marginalized at odds with each other they can continue to pass laws that make our existing unnecessarily difficult. They use misinformation and target Black men because they know that Black men are tired of being scapegoated. Through the spreading of misinformation white supremacists do some of their best work by making Black men feel that the only way for us to achieve any measure of uplift is to take down Black women. As a means of regaining social and financial capital Black men are placed in the compromising position of grasping for anything if it means that we will survive. More decidedly if that surviving means hanging Black women out to dry. This concept is one that I absolutely will not stand behind or support in any way. As Bonilla-Silva (2001) mentions, the domination of not only our bodies but our minds has been made through the keen use of social control. During the period of enslavement whites used their whips, slave patrols, overseers, and other paternalistic practices to keep order and the enslaved in their place (Bonilla-Silva 2001). Now they use misogynoir infused propaganda aimed at continuing to manipulate the most mentally vulnerable. We can each read the reactions on social media and view the success of the anti-Black propaganda and the divide and conquer strategy. What I am often perplexed by is how we all know that white supremacy and anti-Black racism exists and yet we consistently operate as if it does not. There is not one single bootstrap ideology that anti-Black racism did not invent, please let it go.

THE BOOTSTRAPS WERE NOT MADE FOR UPLIFT!

Every time I hear someone mention anything about bootstraps and pulling them up, I already know they have not done the reading. Only African Americans were brought to this country against our will as a colonized people and are still blamed for our condition. Africans were trafficked to work in a social experiment and then their descendants were blamed for not taking advantage of their kidnapping. TF?! No other group of people arrived at America in that way and are still made to feel responsible for their oppression in perpetuity. I often hear Black folks say things like *how long are we going to blame white people for our problems?* Or *when are we going to hold ourselves accountable for our choices?* The mere mention of either of these white supremacy infused talking points sends a shiver of rage down my spine. There will never be a time when the invention of race; white supremacy; enslavement; and anti-Black racism will not be to blame for every single issue that occurs within the Black community. *Full stop!* Knowing who you are means understanding that none of this is our fault. Not the poverty; the missing fathers; the lack of education; or the drugs and violence pushed into our redlined communities. *None of it!*

It has been common practice from the time of Booker T. Washington until present day respectable anti-Black-Black folks who dare to blame the enslaved, formerly enslaved, and their descendants for how they responded to the conditions of their oppression. Washington sought to convince white people that we intended to do them no harm, that we were not vengeful, and that we would remain separate to accommodate their carnal and paternalistic desires for Black subjugation. In Washington's reality the best way to keep white folks at bay is to not bring attention to ourselves in ways that would threaten their way of life and how we appear in opposition to them. The issue with this logic being applauded today is that it fails to place the onus of this treacherous connection where it belongs, with the enslavers and their descendants. Regardless of what African Americans tried to do whether they chose to stay out of the way of white people, or their attempt to assimilate into their dominant culture there was violence. One thing white people loved and love to do is meddle into business and spaces that are not intended for them. However, because of their white racialized category they have been raised to believe that anything they can see, touch, and imagine is theirs for the taking which includes Black peace, solitude, and progress.

Regardless of how well African Americans did for themselves post-enslavement and post-Jim Crow there were always white people clawing at their boots in an attempt to drag them backwards. There have been conversations about rebuilding Black cities and creating spaces solely for us as if those places have not previously existed and met the same end through white racialized violence. The issue has never been African Americans within the context of the American social experiment, this issue has always been racist white people. The bootstraps that people like to reference have been bought, paid for, and stolen from the very people sworn by the masses to not ever have done enough. Knowing who you are means knowing full well that Blackness has always been for sale as has our peace and uplift but not by the majority or the whole of us. Whiteness and the upholders of it which also includes Black and non-Black people of color alike are the folks who believe they deserve the right to dictate who benefits from us and how. Everyone [*not us*] benefits from the same Black culture that they consider ghetto and beneath them. In a recent conversation with a fraternity brother of mine we disagreed on a discussion topic related to the bootstraps logic and blaming Black folks. He passionately and inaccurately expressed his perspectives about our conditions and how it is no longer white people to blame. I encouraged him to read more from Black scholars who have done the working in combating deficit framed perspectives aimed at our continued demonization and he refused. What struck me the most was that he was staunch in his belief that he was correct, and it was in that moment and moments like it that I realize that some of us might be too far gone. Gone as in unsavable from the stain of anti-Black racism and white supremacist ideologies. A heartbreaking reality because at the core of it all I am keenly aware that none of it is their fault even if I disagree with them, and I often do.

In his book *Faces at the bottom of the well: The Permanence of Racism* Derrick Bell (1992) states:

> Black people are the magical faces at the bottom of society's well. Even the poorest whites, those who must live their lives only a few levels above, gain their self-esteem by gazing down on us. Surely, they must know that their deliverance depends on letting down their ropes. Only by working together is escape possible. Over time, many reach out, but most simply watch, mesmerized into maintaining their unspoken commitment to keeping us where we are, at whatever cost to them or us.

What Bell so succinctly states is that the work of Black liberation is a work that is also beneficial to lower class and impoverished white people. The same white people who were only elevated from the bowels of inferiority because they were allowed entrance into the racialized category known as *white* in the first place. What should be an obvious implication for community and com-radery is always a missed opportunity because the social position that white-ness gives them is more important than liberation for us all. Understanding this perspective will help you understand why as a white person saying that you were not privileged or you yourself did not enslave anyone is not the flex that you believe it to be. Many of you are indeed descendants of enslavers and have full working knowledge of it as well as the records that they kept in pristine shape which list the names of our ancestors, yet you keep them. You did not have to own the enslaved to still participate in their continued enslavement even in their death.

Slavery happened in America and the families of the enslavers did not just up and disappear, nor did their records. Part of your role in liberating the descendants of your ancestors is giving us access to know who we are and who we come from in name and in deed. Your role in liberating us as a co-conspirator also means granting us our rights to no longer be shackled to the unknown. You know your people and we absolutely deserve the right to know ours. Whiteness tends to operate with conditions and the conditions in which it operates make it such that anything that threatens its authority is silenced. The descendants of the enslaved Africans in America are owed a great debt from this country and white people know that they are the key to making that happen. The mere fact that white Americans can name their sixth great grandfather and African Americans who have been here just as long and are not able to do the same is a crime against humanity.

BY ANY MEANS NECESSARY!

When I think about the vestiges of enslavement juxtaposed to contemporary society, I often wonder how we manage to remain a peaceful people. We are one of the only colonized groups who will face traumatic occurrences and society just moves along as if nothing occurred. The denial of our experiences consistently intersect with requests of us to be patriotic Americans. Black people are often asked to be the saviors of democracy while everyone else is allowed to focus on their individual groups needs. I am always reminded that the only people that actually have our back is us. It is not healthy to be angry all the time, but it is equally as harmful to live in denial about the reali-ties of our Black existence. In America, it is common for a Black child to be killed by cops or vigilantes and instead of creating legal precedent that disal-lows for the hunting of Black people the country will criminalize the victim. Meanwhile, a white person will kill their entire family and the media will show a photo of them and their victims in happier times. There was a time when I wanted to believe that most of the country were legitimately unaware of anti-Black racism. It was because it was easier to imagine a country full of culturally inept people than for me to fathom that everyone is complicit in our oppression, *what a time!* Fortunately for me, I realized rather quickly that the only thing worse than hoping for the best in white people is actually expecting the best from white people. When you prepare for the violence of whiteness it actually disallows for you to be gravely surprised when they show themselves. This frame of thought does not prevent me from seeing good white people, but it certainly keeps me from expecting it from them. The onus of their anti-racist behavior is not upon me to give them an extension of grace. Instead, the onus rests with them to prove to me why I should. That perspective may not make many of you all happy or feel fuzzy inside but that also is not my or my peoples' cross to bear.

One of the things that I have long realized about understanding my Blackness is that it means releasing myself from the concern of how it looks to other people. In a class that I was teaching I recall a student of mine referring to a time where he was wearing a tank top and a durag while driving to see his father in a nice neighborhood. He said that his dad was really adamant about him looking respectable as he navigated the neighborhood but most likely the world. Our elders have been conditioned to believe that certain attire saves you from death and it is quite frankly still a frustratingly existing point for many of them. Although I am frustrated by their perspectives on what attire makes you worthy of saving, it is not their fault. Today, as I sit here to write these words, I was made aware of the senseless killing of yet another unarmed Black man at the hands of the police. His name is Keenan Anderson, and he was a high school English teacher and a father. I do not believe that you could be a less confrontational person and yet he was still tased to death by LAPD. What I find to be most frustrating about these instances is that there is no job, status symbol, earned degree, or familial connection that can save you when white supremacy comes knocking. Understanding this very depressing reality why are we made to believe that any of the previously mentioned ever could?

We have to arrive at a point on our journey where we reach an understanding that white people at large never intended to grant us our freedom. At large, white people never intended to see us as their equal. At the core of white acceptance is the belief that it [their acceptance] is and will always be needed. Their acceptance is what grants us some sort of immunity in our engagement and relationship with oppression, or so we think. Your immunity from their racism is only good as long as you are in service with and to them. Most white people still have no real investment in seeing liberation for us or seeing a world where they are not classified as most necessary. The most liberal among them still cannot fathom a world where they are not allowed to be the heroes at the end of the story. Whiteness even with its best intentions disallows for those who identify with it to ever fathom a world where people of color are not used for their utility and the pushing of their agenda. My stating, *by any means necessary* is me making it painstakingly clear that with or without the approval of whiteness we must be liberated. We must be liberated because it is the only option.

As Carmichael (1966) stated, in this constant debate over our existence, negroes are dependent on, and exist at the discretion of, a white society which has no investment in our honest and fair representation. Understanding our relationship with the national media and its false interpretation of us as dangerous and uncontrollable in attempt to create race-war mongering (Carmichael 1966), which disallows for objective reporting of racialized incidents. The intention of creating an impenetrable cape of innocence for whiteness and an unshakable cloud of guilt over Blackness is alarming but expected. The only people to ever believe the opposite is true are people who refuse to pay attention or are committed to their version of the story as an indisputable fact.

Carmichael (1966) further posits that this limitation of perceptions and vision are directly related to the censorship of history of both itself and African Americans. Stokely recognized this about the social experiment that is America fifty-seven years ago. This was prior to the *CRT bans*, the *DEI bans*, the *Don't Say Gay bans*, and the ban on the word *Latinx*! Which further brings home the point that I have made throughout this text and that is that the rule book for dividing and conquering those racialized as white and those racialized as Black is effective. The only thing that changes in this game are the cast of characters and the additional moving target aimed at any other marginalized and colonized group. What I find to be among of the many frustrating things that Americans do is pretend to be unaware. The discourse of the elders in white families regarding their racist ideologies is intended to pass the recipes of oppression forward.

Its precisely why sitting silently as your granny or paw-paw spew hateful rhetoric under the auspices that they are old and "settled" in their ways makes you a forever problem. Whereas you might be objectively opposed to their problematic takes there is and will always be someone who finds favor in their beliefs. Their hatred provides a place of comfort for the youth who need to find a place to scapegoat their own mediocrity and thus continuing on in the familial traditions of whiteness and racism. In order for us to move toward liberation we will have to tussle with society for the right to create our ways of being as defined by us and in our own terms (Carmichael 1966). As for me and my house, I will always consider this a well-deserved battle and one that I will gladly take up arms for. We have for far too long been forced to only define ourselves for other people and in their image of us which only continues to harm us in perpetuity. Our divorcing of our terms of knowing and belonging through the guidance and gaze of whiteness is inevitable and requires it to meet its most expedient end. Our being cannot be policed or shaped by the purveyors of our oppression regardless of how kind they show up to us. Our resistance movement much like all of the movements that preceded it are intended to address the oppression of our time (Haynes, et al. 2019). Although many of our experience are mirrored to that of our elders and ancestors one thing remains vastly different and that is *social media.* Social media allows for Gen X, Millennials, and Gen Z to view our experiences with white supremacy and racism from across the country in real time. This is not an avenue that was available to our elders in their youth and for that reason it creates a disconnect with what we see and experience and what they hear and how they advise us.

The advent of social media has allowed for us to organize across state lines and the globe in ways not seen previously. The summer after Breonna Taylor, Ahmaud Arbery, and George Floyd were murdered immediately proved this fact. This is not intended to dismiss global organizational efforts of times past, but it is intended to highlight some of the very unique differences and technological advances that allow for urgent information to be passed within seconds not days or even weeks. What this particular moment in times allows us to see is the performance of equity and the poor application of inclusion among our institutions of higher learning who should be leading the charge (Haynes et al. 2019). Instead of leading the charge for progressivism and equity personified we are watching the radical right wing political pundits drag us backward in higher education and society at large. The fight for our liberation and the democracy of this country is upon us. What matters to me most is that we do not end up losing ourselves and all that we have accomplished in the wake of white carnage and misplaced feelings because of their personal and cultural mediocrity. White people who participate in the oppression of marginalized communities and namely African Americans are content with participating in the harm but hate the idea that anyone else might find out. The use of terms like "cancel culture" and "woke culture" are intended to troll marginalized people for naming and calling out instances of racism and white supremacy. White people are fully aware of social media and how fast the word is passed and so their counterpoint has always been to create a distraction within the disruption to sidetrack as many followers of the movement as possible. The distraction always proves successful, and it is precisely why we need to be aware of not allowing ourselves to be dissuaded from our liberatory efforts.

The greatest threat to the end of white supremacy and anti-Black racism is the uniting of Africa's children. There is no way around us truly being able to walk in our own light without truly accepting who we are and what belongs to us. Once you are committed to the act of knowing there is no distraction worthy of returning to a place of unknowing. Your strength exists within your recognition of the uniqueness of your own Blackness and its ordained responsibility to uplift the uniqueness of others. You lose absolutely nothing simply because you make space for others to exist freely in their own image of themselves. However, you lose everything the moment you begin to orchestrate for other people the ways in which you believe they must exist. Especially if the way that you believe they should exist is in accordance with the rule of white law and Black respectability. As millennials we are unique in because of the way that society has shifted from the time of our youth to adulthood (Allen et al. 2020). We are the most educated generation with Generation Z right behind us (Allen et al. 2020). As a result of our education we have the ability to recognize all the ways that we have been wronged and the courage to address the violation the moment that it occurs. We are not making excuses for the disrespect or allowing grace for the way that white supremacy and anti-Black racism continues to intrude on us or co-opt our culture. We will be liberated . . . *by any means necessary!*

REFERENCES

Bell, Derrick. 1992. *Faces At The Bottom Of The Well: The Permanence of Racism.* New York: Basic Books.

Black, Wayne, Frederick Engram, and Travis Smith. 2022. *It was NEVER about Deion: HBCU Realities VS. Perceptions.* December 22. https://www.diverseeducation.com/opinion/article/15304603/it-was-never-about-deion-hbcu-realities-vs-perceptions.

Bonilla-Silva, Eduardo. 2001. *White Supremacy & Racism in the Post-Civil Rights Era.* Boulder: Lynne Rienner.

Carmichael, Stokely. 1966. "Toward Black Liberation." *SNCC* 639–651.

Cross, William E. 1981. "Black Families and Black Identity Development; Rediscovering the Distinction Between Self-esteem and Reference Group Orientation." *Journal of Comparative Family Studies Vol. 12 No.1* 19–49.

Dei, George J. Sefa. 2017. *Reframing Blackness and Black Solidarities through Anti-Colonial and Decolonial Prisms.* Toronto: Springer.

Hatter, Lynn. 2019. *The Repeating History Behind The Closure Of Florida A&M University's Hospital.* November 22. https://news.wfsu.org/wfsu-local-news/2019-11-22/the-repeating-history-behind-the-closure-of-florida-a-m-universitys-hospital.

Haynes, Chayla, Milagros Castillo-Montoya, Meseret Hailu, and Saran Stewart. 2019. "Black Deprivation, Black Resistance, and Black Liberation: the influence of #BlackLivesMatter (BLM) on higher education." *International Journal of Qualitative Studies in Education* 1067–1071.

Jenkins, DeMarcus. 2021. "Unspoken Grammar of Place: Anti-Blackness as a Spatial Imaginary in Education." *Journal of School Leadership* 107–126.

Lindsey, Treva. 2020. *The urgent crisis of missing Black women and girls.* February 20. https://womensmediacenter.com/news-features/the-urgent-crisis-of-missing -black-women-and-girls.

Shaonta' E. Allen, Ifeyinwa F. Davis,Maretta McDonald,Candice C. Robinson. 2020. "The Case of Black Millennials." *Sociological Approaches to Millennials Vol 63 Issue 3* 478–485.

Chapter 3

A Change is Gonna Come

MY CHILDHOOD AS A MODEL TEMPLATE

As a child, I recall fondly how my mother was always a stickler for education. When the academic year commenced, and most of our peers began planning their summer escapades of days filled with bike riding, hide-and-go-seek, freeze tag, and even knock-knock scramble. My siblings and I knew that the only part of our schooling that would end is the part where we had to make our daily commute to our public school. Instead, our real education was about to begin. Before we even dared to dart our doorstep to join our friends in summer-time shenanigans mom would take us to the public library. Once we arrived at the library, we were tasked with locating ten books that piqued our interest. My mother was very clear that we were not allowed to grab what she considered to be "easy" books. Easy books were considered books that were quick reads, not historically significant, or were not considered advanced enough for our reading level. My mother was adamant that we grabbed books steeped in Black history and books that told our stories differently than what we were taught in school or not taught at all.

I would grab books that told biographical and historical stories about our Black heroes and heroines. Books about great Black figures such as Crispus Attucks, George Washington Carver, Harriet Tubman, Sojourner Truth, and Mary McCleod Bethune. Each of these books provided more for me than I could ever imagine. For starters, it provided for me historical underpinnings of the Black lived experience in America. It also helped to build my confidence in understanding who I was and from whence we came. My older brother was never a fan of the readings and often complained that they were "boring." I could not disagree more and instead of rejecting what my mother was intending to instill in me I leaned into it. As a ten-year-old I became enthralled by our stories and the only thing that could satisfy my hunger aside from readings were historical films. *Race to Freedom* which starred Dawn Lewis, Courtney B. Vance, Glynn Turman and others was my first visual introduction to the enslavement of Africans in America when I was just eleven years old. My maternal grandparents were watching it on the Family Channel, and I became enamored by the resilience of our people and the fire that they each held within. It was this film in 1994, that stoked my ever-burning fire for understanding Black American history within the context of forced enslavement and their fight for liberation. I recall my brothers' resistance and hesitation toward watching this film and his voice still echoes today whenever I hear our people state that they do not need to see another slave movie or hear about it. At the age of eleven, I was still wise enough to know that evading the truth of our toiled history would not change it and that refusing to learn about it would not erase its existence and ever-present persistence. My mother was single-handedly responsible for teaching me about anti-Blackness through practice through no fault of her own as well as providing me the tools I would later need to mentally liberate myself from it.

In my youth I was able to contextualize what I was watching and make sense of how it related to our current experience. I was able to begin to make sense of racism and I dared not shy away from difficult discussions or viewings if it would provide me some form of enlightenment. My mothers' determination to make certain that my siblings and I did not grow up unaware or ill prepared to deal with racism in our day-to-day life cannot be understated. I can recall my mothers' difficulty in existing in a professional white world that told Black women how to exist. My siblings and I knew if mom beat us home from work that she likely had a bad day. All we needed to do was eavesdrop on conversations between her and her close girlfriends or our grandparents. From these seemingly secretive discussions we were able to confirm that mom either quit her job or was let go. Admittedly as a child, I was not always able to make sense of what my mother was experiencing and or deduct who was immediately at fault. However, I do recall instances where she insinuated that her employers in fact "*had the wrong one.*" That statement is code for someone making the mistake of speaking to her in a way that she considered disrespectful and disparaging. As a Black woman, my mother often faced instances of misogynoir (Bailey and Trudy 2018), and she was expected to take it on the chin. I realized early on that there was only one way to deal with racism and that was head on. In an incident when we were playing Pop Warner football in my hometown of Utica, New York I remember a situation where a white coach threw my older brother to the ground. It was in frustration because my brother was not running the play correctly and he grew tired of repeating the route to him. My mother received word that this large immature white man put his hands on her child and without as much as a second thought she drove her car onto the football field intending on running him over. When she retold the story, she mentioned seeing red at the idea of a white man placing his hands upon her child with or without cause. Someone reading this might consider that response immature or unnecessary which is easy to say if you are not Black, a mother, and a protector. My mother taught us by her actions with or without intending to, exactly how to tackle racism whenever it appeared and that was directly. When I think about liberation, I view it in three parts: *(1) what does liberation look like? (2) how do we get out of our own way? And (3) bringing others along.*

A CHANGE *MUST* COME!

Sam Cooke's *A Change is Gonna Come* provided an anthem for the Civil Rights movement of the 1960s. From the intro of the song with the strings blaring to Sam's declaration of where he was born, and that change has been coming for quite a while. He uses the song to tell a story about his struggles with finding the strength to carry on as African Americans battled white supremacy. A feeling and experience that is all too familiar to many of our parents and grandparents who were alive during that time. The feeling of rage, hopelessness, and determination all flowing through their veins. As they simply desired to exist free from the reign of white terror and afforded the opportunity to make a peaceful and equitable life for themselves and their children. An existence that has long been denied for our people since we arrived on the shores of this unfamiliar place against our will. As a people we constantly find ourselves embattled with controversy over topics relating to our freedom and right to live as we see fit. We are forever entrenched with white people demanding that we explain how or why we choose to engage with them and when. White people have always considered themselves to be the ambassadors of our American existence even when they refuse to acknowledge it.

To paint a more vivid picture I will state that the actions and sometimes inaction of whiteness further cements my previous statement. White women using their physical being to demand that we explain to them who we are, where we are going, and to prove that we belong. White women are an audacious species because on one hand they rally against patriarchy while using their other hand to hold back Black women and women of color. How can you be aware of the torment of white supremacy which birthed patriarchy and in the same breath use your voice to be a willing participant in the continued oppression of African Americans. The answer is quite simple, the womb of white supremacy belongs to white women. Their tears, faux fragility, and manipulative demeanor are their weapons of choice. They actively engage in white supremacy as long as it benefits them even if it means voting against their own self-interests. At the end of the day whiteness will always be the cloak that all white people hide behind until they choose differently. To be clear, before the faux outrage starts and people become distracted let me speak directly and say that I do not hate white women. I do, however, despise white supremacy!

White people have a choice to make every day when they wake up. They can choose to reject their whiteness and use their privilege to benefit the historically disenfranchised or they can pretend to be obtuse. Whiteness and its privilege are the gifts that keep on giving and no amount of denying it will ever change that. It is one of the most alarming things about what has occurred regarding faux allyship during the pandemic following the murder of George Floyd by former police officer Derek Chauvin. There were bare shelves at bookstores because of the heavy influx of white guilt that made their false sense of allyship seem legitimate. From the painting of sidewalks to the murals, and removal of confederate statues all of it was performative. Some of those same people who pretended to care about the constant loss of Black lives turned around and voted against the best interest of those same lives during the November 2020 election. I refuse to believe that only the publicly racist supporters of the previous administration and its apologists are the only people who supported his re-election or those who stormed the Capitol on January 6th, 2021. History constantly reminds us to be cautious of well-intentioned whiteness and to be in a constant state of critiquing white liberalism (Bansal and Bell 1988).

One of the harsh realities that I also discovered during the pandemic and in the wake of George Floyd's murder is the number of African American apologists. Civil unrest will always be the result of any unjustified loss of life at the hands of the state. Yet, elder African Americans knowing full well that liberation does not come without loss are requiring of justifiably angry young people to be still. As Dr. King once told us that a riot (civil unrest) is a response of the unheard. If we are all clear that marginalized groups, a community that they hold membership in are the unheard why is it so hard to fathom that the unheard would eventually rise up?

The intimate yet unrequited relationship between African Americans and the police is unlike any other systemic relationship in this country. This does not discount any of the other marginalized groups and their engagement with the police. However, none of the other groups have a relationship that began due to the enslavement of Africans in this country. The traumatic and uninvited relationship that exists between the two is one that will never be beneficial to African Americans. Understanding this dichotomous relationship will also help any observer in understanding why there will never be complete peace between the two. No matter how many of us that decide to suit up in blue we will never be treated or valued the same way that they view and value whiteness. One of the core misunderstandings of Black people who enter the field of policing is that they honestly believe that they can change the scope of policing from the inside out. What many of them fail to realize is that policing is a system rooted in the oppression of Blackness. Unless the entire system is abolished no amount of negro infusing will make a difference. You may change the face of white violence, but the violence is still in fact, *white*.

The discussion of whether or not to abolish policing is one that is controversial between African Americans. This is largely because as African Americans we have not ever experienced an existence free from white rule. When you have a country that instills the idea that policing is an inevitable good and that people cannot police themselves it creates doubt in the minds of many. This concept rings true for many elders in the African American community who lived during the crack era where intragroup violence seemed incapable of resolve. Many of those same elders, elected officials, clergy men and women all played a role in the passing of the Crime Bill in 1994. What many of them failed to realize is that agreeing to support such a horrendous bill would prove detrimental to the African American community when it single-handedly created a prison boom. The same prison boom that would rip apart Black families, send Black children into foster care, create a larger separation of the wealth gap, and increase the over-policing of Black and Latinx communities. Policing much like the period of enslavement that it evolved from has never and will never be good for African Americans or other communities of color. *Period!*

WHITENESS AS A FORM OF POLICING

Policing in its current form is not solely restricted to police officers it has become synonymous with white people who see America as their own personal playground and everyone else as trespassers (Harris 1993). White people police all aspects of America even in spaces where they are very clearly out of bounds (Engram 2021). The core belief that America belongs to white people has long since been the attitude of the majority group. A group that feels that they are above rules and that rules are only intended to keep their power structure current and the oppressed people, oppressed. White people have done a good job of stating that this is not the case while simultaneously staging insurrections, passing racist voting laws, subjugating women [*even elected ones*], and restricting the teaching of actual American history. If white people and the GOP are good at nothing else, they are good at the tactic of bait and switch. Meaning that they will be intentional about causing you harm all while using white tears to proclaim that it is in fact you who is causing harm to them (Comer 1969). We have witnessed this with Amy Cooper who used white feminism to intentionally cause harm to Christian Cooper in Central Park or the countless white women who used their bodies and voices to instill fear into the unsuspecting Black person. It is an action that is prevalent in K-12 classrooms, on college campuses, and in the workplace. White violence and the purveyors of it are literally everywhere.

The unwavering sting of whiteness and its privilege is that it gives its beneficiaries an option (Zuberi and Bonilla-Silva 2008). A white person could actively choose to reject their privilege and begin to use it to serve the marginalized. It can also be used by white persons who even with mediocre skills and credentials will still have a better chance at wealth accumulation as millennials than my African American peers and myself. Regardless of how educated my peers and I become we will never be able to shake the reality of our collective history. Largely because the world has been overrun by white supremacy and we are not allowed to forget it. As we continue to think more broadly about the need for change it must be considered just how widespread white supremacy is. As previously mentioned, K-12, higher education, and the workplace are places of comfort for the violence of whiteness. This is largely due to the fact that each of these organizational structures were initially created to be of service to white men and eventually white women. All of these structures were not intended to be inclusive of African American men, women, or children.

LIBERATION AS AN ACTION: MOVE!

The first step toward liberation is rooted in understanding and not avoiding the truth of the past. Although white supremacy is not nor has it ever been our responsibility; how we learn from it, is. White supremacy has created centuries of separation between all Black people and has caused us to create a faux sense of hierarchy among our own people. Whether it be who is Black enough; if non-descendants of enslaved Africans can claim Blackness; or if biracial or white passing Black people should be able to be labeled Black. All of the infighting keeps us from being on one accord and focusing on how to liberate us all. This was the intention of white supremacy since its inception. Confusion and mayhem have always been the aim because with confusion and mayhem people can easily lack focus and vision. In order to understand how to liberate ourselves we have to be humble enough to learn how we arrived at this point. We know white supremacy has long been the responsible culprit and offender that causes us racial victimization. However, we owe it to ourselves to no longer allow white supremacy and racists to tell our stories. Understanding that Blackness is not monolithic is one thing but also understanding that your version of Blackness is not the only version that matters, is heightened awareness. An awareness that all of our stories deserve to be told is how we begin to move toward liberation. Breaking free from social constructs designated for and by whiteness, forced upon and later adopted by everyone else as a norm must be countered. The ideology and legal framing of whiteness (Harris 1993) sets a tone of social correctness based upon eurocentrism not traditional African culture.

A system not rooted in helping us to succeed but a system rooted in and benefiting from our oppression. As African Americans we often find ourselves having to defend our truth in regard to racism which is a form of white supremacy. We have witnessed recent occurrences of this same gaslighting aimed at Black athletes like Simone Biles, Serena Williams, Naomi Osaka, or Kyrie Irving. Each of whom have prioritized their mental health above the expectation of others. Whiteness as property was coined by CRT scholar and Law Professor Cheryl I. Harris. Professor Harris provided us a scholarly way to understand how whiteness is viewed in the world and its benefit. Professor Harris (1993) tells us the story of her grandmother who out of a desperate need to provide for her children chose to "pass." White-passing is a term used to describe how fair-skin African Americans publicly denied their Blackness in an attempt to create an existence that would be comparable to white Americans. It was a practice that took place during and after reconstruction where many African Americans were simply trying to find a way to peacefully exist (Harris 1993). It was not a decision that one could make without full consideration of what the revealing of their truth could mean. It often required fair-skin African Americans to separate themselves from their more physically noticeable African American relatives. It is the untold story of far too many American families who had a secretly Black grandmother or grandfather who passed so they could survive the oppressive social experiment that is America.

As told by Harris (1993), her grandmother shared in this silent kinship of many African Americans who made this traumatic decision. Harris speaks of her grandmother's trauma in revisiting when racist comments were said in her presence because they believed that she would mirror their sentiments. She knew all too well that the price of her decision meant that her decision bought her silence. Professor Harris' article, investigated the complicated relationship between both race and property and how the two are intertwined. As we view this very entangled relationship between the two, we must also consider the historical forms of domination that are connected to the present. Harris (1993) stated that the racial subordination of African Americans and Native Americans, and the racialization of identity provided the ideological basis for conquest and enslavement. Although each of their systemic oppression differed in form—the former involving the appropriation and seizure of

labor, the latter entailing the appropriation and seizure of land—undergird-
ing both was a racialized conception of property ratified by law and imple-
mented by force (Harris 1993). What we see on college campuses as well as
in public spaces and to be more specific predominately white institutions are
the actions of this core CRT concept. White Americans have been raised to
believe that any space that they occupy even if temporarily, is their space.
This belief is only further reinforced when other non-white people are present. White people at large share this same global concept which is indicative
of how widespread white supremacy is. Jeff Bezos and Richard Branson
are both the latest versions of this concept where white men feel that space
should also be colonized. There does not seem to exist a lane that whiteness
dares not swerve into. Whiteness is a system that we are all policed by against
our will by both foundational law and reinforcement. Understanding this reality, how could any American who is not a beneficiary of this value system
disagree about its harm and existence.

At every turn in the United States, African Americans find themselves
being undervalued, undercompensated, and overworked and this applies
to all educational levels. Regardless of our levels of education and work
experience we will never be able to rid ourselves of how white people view
our Blackness. Very similar to our more recent elders who used passing as
a means of survival, we have African Americans who have amassed various
levels of success who choose to use their status in these spaces as a means
of separating themselves from other marginalized members of their same
group. We have witnessed this behavior displayed among athletes, actors,
rappers, and even your favorite academics. Whiteness has always been used
as the barometer in which success and proximity to it is determined. Not
understanding the role of white supremacy in our daily existence makes
people feel that being accepted by it as opposed to destroying it is the better option (Black, Engram, and Smith 2022). Those same individuals will
often use some of the same tactics as an intragroup measurement of success
or worthiness. Harris (1993), further explains that property rights within the
United States have always been rooted in the domination of certain races. At
the inception of this nation, it was not the concept of race alone that operated
to oppress Native Americans and the enslaved; rather, it was the *interaction*
between conceptions of property and race that played a critical role in estab-
lishing and maintaining economic and racial subordination (Harris 1993).

HYPER EXPLOITATION AND OBJECTIFICATION

For those of us who are scholar-practitioners, educators, skilled-laborers, or
situated within any other possible discipline or industry we are all well-versed

in being exhausted by our place of employment. Just when you think that it is not possible to be labored any further someone says, "hold my beer." Black labor being hyper-exploited has often been accomplished by treating Black people themselves as objects of property. This problematic undertaking allowed for the conflating of race and property which established a form of property being solely contingent upon race—only (Harris 1993). Black people were treated as property and subjugated to being enslaved. Harris (1993) explains that the further exploitation of native lands allowed for white people to seize and occupy those lands further making whiteness a privilege and constructing whiteness as actual property. Racial hierarchy has long been a standing structure within this country which was established during chattel slavery and reinforced today. The rules that were established in this country were never created to police white people. Laws have always been established to keep the supremacy of whiteness as the ruling class and the supreme decision-making authority.

According to Harris (1993), the social construction of the white identity as well as the ideology of racial hierarchy are intimately tied to the expansion and evolution of chattel slavery. Viewing the dominant paradigm of social relations at that time proved something very intentional, and that is that although not all Africans were enslaved, virtually all of the enslaved were not white. The obvious rationale for the enslavement of Africans was due to their racialized othering (Harris 1993).This same mindset is what we march for all of these years later. As we witnessed on January 6, 2021, white people became aggrieved by the mere concept that it was the Black vote that shifted the United States 2020 election cycle. They became so enraged that they began demanding that votes in largely Black districts either be re-counted to their satisfaction or completely disregarded. The caucacity of this assertion is quite astounding. White people have been so used to having everything go their way that when it did not, they literally and figuratively tried to dismantle the government and procedures that they themselves created.

During the Black Lives Matter protests of 2020, we watched in real time the ugliness of the relationship between Black people, co-conspirators, and the police. We all witnessed the vicious attacks on unarmed American citizens solely because they were standing up for the rights of Black people and appropriately saying, fuck police brutality! Not nearly an entire calendar year later, we watched on every news station how privilege works. As I sat in my living room on my sofa awaiting the certification of President Biden and Vice President Kamala Harris' victory, I witnessed in real time the horror of the January 6th insurrection. I still do not have the words to describe what I witnessed but I know that I was frozen in place. We were witnessing cops being hugged and kissed in one camera shot, replacing their required attire with MAGA wear, and being bludgeoned in another camera shot. All while guns remained holstered and the national guard and all other authorities were asked to stay away. If that is not considered privilege, I shudder to think what exactly would meet the burden of that proof. The preponderance of evidence was very clear on CNN, MSNBC, and FOX News yet the then lame duck now ex-president and his cronies are still trying to convince us otherwise.

When we speak of change in this country, we are specifically discussing the inequitable balance of power. The concept that whiteness deserves all manner of forgiveness and everyone else are not provided that same level of grace. A heavy-handed justice system that would punish a Black mother for enrolling her child in a different school district but will slap the hand of a white man or woman who commits treason is not an equity driven or blind justice system. Change is determined by what is right and just for every living being despite any of our differences and not one that is solely advantageous for whiteness. The United States, local and national government, institutions of higher learning, K-12, and corporations all make strides for Blackness when there is some benefit to whiteness (Bell 1980). This concept is referred to as interest convergence and it is also a tenet of critical race theory.

CONVERGENCE OF WHITE INTERESTS AT BLACK COSTS

As a secondary to understanding the role of whiteness and its proximity to power we must also understand the role of converging interests and how to get out of our own way. Interest convergence as described by Derrick Bell (1980), helps us to understand that decisions regarding equity should not be determined solely if they are advantageous to white people. Understanding equitable treatment means understanding that even if the least of us benefit than the most of us will also benefit. The United States and privileged white people have not yet grasped this concept. To them, any benefit to any marginalized group is somehow a loss to the majority group and that could not be more asininely selfish. When you are so accustomed to your own privilege anything that does not seem favorable to you feels like oppression. I often compare whiteness and the beneficiaries of it to petulant children and the only people who I owe an apology to are the children. History has shown us that white people respond at the slightest hint of an inconvenience with rage and violence. All while simultaneously finding zero issue with punching down on those who they marginalize and offering no understanding or support of the historically disenfranchised. After the summer of 2020, we began to witness performative allyship all across the United States. We witnessed the removal of confederate statues, the changing names of buildings on white college campuses, and the renaming of streets all over the country. What we did not witness was a mass change in police brutality or the dismissal of qualified immunity. The renaming and removal of buildings and statues benefits whiteness because it allows the elected officials or school administrators who are making the decisions to look like heroes. Black people and well-intentioned white people alike called these juvenile steps "a start," and I am always enraged by such small mindedness. When we become easily distracted by shiny objects it allows for us to be out of tune in regard to the bigger issues. What we need is accountability from our elected officials and those who are hired to serve and protect, and we still need to abolish it all and start over. As African Americans in a country that our ancestors built with their blood, sweat, and tears all we have ever received are crumbs and most white people believe even that is too much.

The mere fact that every good thing that African Americans and other communities of color receive is because wealthy white people agree with it is interest convergence. The beginning of the pandemic found our elected officials split on issues of aiding their struggling constituents. People who have free healthcare and bloated salaries are the deciding factor as to whether the people who they keep impoverished deserve a living wage or their own money to help them stay afloat. Once a decision was passed that would minimally help their constituents, they applauded themselves for doing a good deed. If you are not personally and currently affected by impoverished living and working conditions, it is not equitable for you to be an expert or spokesperson on what the affected should do. The United States much like colleges and universities creates a faux sense of diversity, equity, and inclusivity with words that are consistently misaligned with reality. If majority white groups are making decisions regarding communities of color, you should always be skeptical. If you are not skeptical of decision makers who are not actively engaged with and have membership within marginalized communities, you are not paying attention. Many will argue that you do not have to hold membership in those communities to advocate for them. As a member of marginalized communities, I wholeheartedly disagree. Even as an African American man, I do not claim to know everything about African American women who are cis or transgender. That would be presumptive of me to even assert that I could remotely understand the issues that they face. Therefore, it is unfathomable for me to believe that white people with plush salaries and epic fringe benefits could ever understand, me. Part of getting out of our own way is admitting when we are misaligned in our beliefs in comparison to what is just, morally right, and equitable for the more marginalized among us.

As mentioned by Bell (1980), some white people may agree that African Americans are citizens and are entitled to constitutional protection against discrimination based upon race. However, few are willing to recognize that segregation based upon race is much more than a series of quaint customs that can be easily remedied without affecting them. To further understand white people's unwillingness to be equitable, we can take a look at affirmative action programs that require white people to step aside to make space for African Americans who they consider less deserving. Many of us have witnessed the mediocrity of whiteness especially within the academy being leapfrogged based upon nepotism. As an African American academic, I like many of my peers, have to go above and beyond to make space for ourselves and others. Meanwhile, being white and male for many is sufficient enough to grant them entrance into the academy. For those of us who are Black and doctoral holders, we understand that the rules do not bend for us even a little. However, almost all of us can tell you a story and provide concrete examples of how that same rule absolutely does not apply to white people.

CUE THE DISRUPTION

Part of being a true disruptor of oppressive systems means understanding that there could be economic or professional losses as a result. The more you cling to the idea that whiteness does not call for disruption or pushback then you have accepted an unworthy fate. This is also an attribute of not getting out of the way of your own advanced learning. This is also the line that separates millennials and gen-z from our gen-x and boomer parents. The latter two generations recognize the role of white supremacy and the harm that it consistently perpetuates across the world. This awakening is not only an awakening of Black and Brown youth as an example. White children, teenagers, and young adults are also starting to question some of the value systems of their families. Generation-Z and TikTok have proven to be a powerful tool for good and for bad. I do not aim to promote TikTok or white youth as the saviors of our democracy, but I will acknowledge that many of them are engaging their racist parents in dialogue that their parents cannot easily run away from. Similar to the ridiculous debate over critical race theory is the debate over the necessary nature of white privilege. As we have each witnessed over the last year, white privilege has proven itself to be unstable, violent, and self-serving. Understanding this reality should make anyone question why whiteness is allowed to be the measurement for all of humanity. The pandemic, insurrection, war on critical race theory, women's reproductive health, and the 1619 project have all reinforced how ridiculously stupid white supremacy is. All of the people who espouse white supremacy and hateful rhetoric make absolutely no sense and many of the children of those people are also recognizing it. However, I do believe that the white youth who are changing their mindsets are very much so in the minority of their ethnic group.

As Bell (1980) highlights for us, even when white people begin to change their mind about the maltreatment of African Americans there is still some benefit to them. Very similarly to when white people realized that enslavement was wrong morally, that value system was still insufficient in regard to bringing about any desired racial reform. In short, white people feeling bad for how their relatives treated us did not and still does not mean a damn thing. Being a co-conspirator, requires for white people to do more than feel bad and to engage in the fight even when there is nothing for them to gain. As a white person who chooses to fight for the liberation of others you must make peace with loss. The loss of friends, family members, social status, and your freedom—temporarily should be expected. If you have not accepted that the liberation of the marginalized will cost you and that you are perfectly fine with it, then you are not ready to stand alongside those of us actively fighting for our liberation. As descendants of the enslaved we do not get the option of picking and choosing which part of our liberation should be up for grabs. We are tasked with fighting for the liberation and value of all Black lives. If this is not your core belief as a non-Black person but you consider yourself an "ally" you my friend have more work to do.

This is why I fundamentally do not believe in allyship when it pertains to race and racism. It for me often boils down to a few fine points, most allyship is performative, rooted in white guilt, and centered in making themselves feel better. It is also situational because it allows for them to pick and choose when to enter the battle for our liberation. It also does not require for them to give up much because they can tweet "Black Lives Matter," post black squares on Instagram, or pay for the lunch of an unsuspecting group of Black folks brunching then return home to their right-wing supporting spouse. True co-conspiratorship as learned from Professor Bettina Love (2020), requires of non-Black persons to agitate the racist people in their lives with points of introspection. If you are someone who even on your best day do all that you can to avoid conflict, you are not a co-conspirator. Being a co-conspirator requires of you to be fearless in the face of racism and it might also require of you to use your physical being to protect a non-white person. It is not a second thought it is an immediate reaction to protect the life of someone other than your own.

During the protests of 2020, I recall an instance in Louisville where a group of white protesters used their bodies as a barrier between the police and Black protesters. I recall another instance that summer when protesters encountered U.S. Park Police. A young Black man approached the police and kneeled with his hands up and the police armed with batons and shields began to approach him. In that instance, a young white woman jumped in front of him and used her body to shield him from police contact. That is the only acceptable method of being a co-conspirator that rises to the same level of white aggression. There is no amount of reading that you could ever do to prepare you for the moment when you are forced to immediately react. Being a co-conspirator, also requires advocating for equity everywhere that inequitable practices are present. It also requires of you to make space for other identities that you may not identify with, but you understand that liberation is also their just due. Educational spaces require the most disruption because as we have witnessed over the past few years that is where white rage has the most immediate and long-term impact. There is no space more deeply rooted in white supremacy than public education. The local control and maintenance of community concern have been the standard in maintaining the status-quo. We have always witnessed what white rage produces and the first place that they run when they feel that there is any level of threat toward the status-quo. One thing is for certain and that is that racist white folks are always predictable, and they are always on time. If you look at pictures of enraged white racists in the 60s and today the only thing that has changed is their clothing and the photograph filter.

Understanding the nuanced relationship between the marginalized, the oppressors, and politics I will always sit in critique of whiteness as an advocate for the marginalized. White people will assert that my hesitancy to trust them or their methods aimed at assisting the marginalized makes me a reverse racist. What is unfortunate for them and anyone who is reading this and believes the same is that that is not even considerable in the closest realm of possibilities. My speaking about whiteness and those who benefit from it is not rooted in fallacy or any desire to make white people look bad. It is rooted in being critical of how white people have displayed themselves throughout history as it pertains to the marginalized. There has never been a time in history where African Americans constructed race, subjugated white people, and legalized our own Blackness with the intention of creating laws aimed at anti-miscegenation. If that had occurred then perhaps I, and other African Americans who do this work could be considered racist. Understanding that white people constructed race within the United States should help others to rationalize that as the social constructers of race they hold the rights to the power and privilege of its assignment. Furthermore, they own the power of its weaponization and who would and should be subjugated by it. Marginalized group members specifically African Americans and Native Nations can be upholders of white supremacy and enact it as an outsider. However, as descendants of the enslaved in this country you have the freedom to be bigoted or prejudice but you, under any circumstance, cannot be racist. The construction of race was an act aimed at being exclusive and separatist and the enslaved had no dog in that fight.

As mentioned by Bansal and Bell (1988), and what absolutely contradicts the media spin on Black liberation movements is this truth, regardless of what Black people say nothing will change the mind of white peoples' determination to maintain a dominant power. At any cost to the life and limb of Black folks, white people will lie simply because they have the legal right to do so granted to them by the color of their skin. Skepticism is a necessary response for people of color who are grappling with political concepts and trusting white people. As a third point on moving towards liberation is for us to be in constant critique of not just liberalism but political ideology as a whole. Being in critique and asking the tough and critical questions allows us to engage individuals with different mentalities than us. This is how we are able to begin to bring others along with us as we disrupt the status-quo and push forward toward liberation. The republican and democrat parties have both been the deciding factors in perpetuating harm in regard to the enslaved, formerly enslaved, and their descendants. No political affiliation in this country has ever made it their business to lift the descendants of enslavement out of poverty, remove the targets placed on us because of our Blackness, or to relentlessly push toward reparations to provide us a fighting chance in perpetuity. Instead, each of the political affiliations use our votes to coax us toward their own agendas aimed at beating the other; and then ditch us in the wake of their victory celebrations. Understanding the political power that Black people have as a collective you would think that the democrats and republicans would fight harder to maintain our right to vote and to work with us.

We constantly find ourselves as the pawn at the fingertips of white possibilities. Forgotten about most of the year and during most administrations only to be remembered during election cycles when pandering is at its greatest height. As discussed by Bell in critical race theory and understood by critical race theorists, racism requires sweeping and immediate changes. Yet, we are often asked by politicians of the most well-intentioned kind to be patient. We are constantly asked to trust them and to allow them to work on our behalf. Meanwhile, as we are practicing patience another fourteen year old was gunned down by the police, a Black mother has lost custody of her children, and a Black father is battling with the courts to expunge his record so that he can adequately provide for his family. Someone might read this and immediately point to these individuals as deserving of their fates. Very rarely do those same people take an honest inventory of the systemic inequality that created each of the aforementioned scenarios. Some Black folks are often guilty of indulging in these same tropes. Believing that racism and racist acts are one-offs allows for well-intentioned white people to further assert that patience be the norm. However, those of us who are closest to the struggle understand that another minute gone is another minute loss and that minute could make the difference in a persons' life.

As the current and immediate past news cycles have shown us that when white people are exempt from racial designations and become "students," "teachers," "families," and "jurors" their ability to see and understand CRT is limited. Further investigating that white people have been the main beneficiaries of civil rights legislation and government assistance should provide some brevity on the matter. Alas, it is easier to pretend that the "welfare queens" and "superpredators" are lurking in the shadows awaiting their opportunity to take advantage of the government. Rather than recognizing that the social conditioning and intentional reinforcement of poverty are what white supremacy looks like when it is legalized and government assistance is weaponized. Not to mention that the true "welfare queens" were white women raising white children and that the notion of "superpredators" as a forthcoming and unavoidable issue was an aggressively racist lie pushed by the beneficiaries of copaganda (Bonilla-Silva 2001).

ACTIVATE LIBERATION AND
DEACTIVATE OPPRESSION

For change to occur we have to get real on what the issues are. For far too long we have been in the weeds as a community distracted by them instead of focusing on who planted them. All of this has been intentional and none of it is ever done without fully recognizing who the least of us are and who will be forced take it on the chin. White people do not stand to gain anything if Black people are liberated and that is why the process has been slow and certainly not steady. The debt owed to us as a people should haunt every leader of this "allegedly" free world every single day. I want liberation not just for me, intersectional feminists, or CRT-theorists, not just for straight or queer people, but for every last one of us because it is what is owed to us. I will not accept any other "feature" and I will not stop telling the truth until the truth becomes the norm. Considering all three components previously mentioned allow for us to paint a picture of what moving towards liberation as millennials should look like. The civil unrests of 2020 as a result of countless killings of unarmed Black people was an opportunity for us all to reimagine what is needed for liberation to occur. Many of my peers and the generation just under us are not intimately familiar with critical race theory, intersectionality, or other critical theoretical frameworks because they are largely academic. We have an opportunity as scholars and millennials to provide easily digestible material intended not for the white gaze but for our own understanding. The consideration of how we reimagine communities that are divested from policing must be on our agenda. Understanding that policing has never prevented crime and that over-policing only aims to target people of color which should be grounds for police nullification at the local levels. If we remove the centrality of white supremacy from our country and our borders, we then remove the need for crime, criminality, and the labeling of deviancy to exist. As we look back on what we have learned regarding whiteness as property, interest convergence, and the critique of politics through the lens of the three liberatory steps. We have to be diligent in our work to apply these realistic practices and amplifying the need for the dissolution of white supremacy as a ruling body.

REFERENCES

Bailey, Moya, and Trudy. 2018. "On misogynoir: citation, erasure, and plagiarism." *Feminist Media Studies Vol. 18 No. 4* 762–768.

Bansal, Preeta, and Derrick Bell. 1988. "The Republican Revival and Racial Politics." *The Yale Law Journal Vol. 97 No.8* 1609–1621.

Bell, Derrick. 1980. "Brown v. Board of Education and the Interest-Convergence Dilemma." *Harvard law Review Vol. 93 No. 3* 518–533.

Black, Wayne, Frederick Engram, and Travis Smith. 2022. *It was NEVER about Deion: HBCU Realities VS. Perceptions.* December 22. https://www.diverseeducation.com/opinion/article/15304603/it-was-never-about-deion-hbcu-realities-vs-perceptions.

Bonilla-Silva, Eduardo. 2001. *White Supremacy & Racism in the Post-Civil Rights Era.* Boulder: Lynne Rienner.

Comer, James P. Dec. 1969. "White Racism: Its Root, Form, and Function." *American Journal of Psychiatry Vol. 126 Issue 6* 777–916.

Harris, Cheryl I. 1993. "Whiteness as property." *Harvard Law Review Vol 106 No.8* 1707–1791.

Jr., Frederick V. Engram. 2021. "White Manning." In *Blackmaled By Academia*, by Gabriele Strohschen, K.B. Elazier and 18 Brave Men, 42–48. Atlanta: American Scholars Press.

Love, Bettina. 2020. *Education Week.* June 12. Accessed September 17, 2022. https://www.edweek.org/leadership/opinion-an-essay-for-teachers-who-understand-racism-is-real/2020/06.

Zuberi, Tukufu, and Eduardo Bonilla-Silva. 2008. *White Logic, White Methods: Racism and Methodology.* Lanham: Rowman & Littlefield.

Chapter 4

Fight the Power!

Respectability and Internalized Anti-Blackness

FIGHT THE POWER!

1980s rap group Public Enemy dropped this anthem in 1989. This song was used to encourage us to use our freedom of speech to fight against our oppression. Part of our liberation work must include encouraging each other to learn how white supremacy has infiltrated the culture. In order for Black people to rid ourselves of the ideologies of whiteness and politics of respectability it must be learned that each of these behaviors stem from white supremacy. White supremacy has been so successful because it causes the oppressed to become upholders of it, if they have not decolonized the way that they view the world. A constant argument that I find myself having with elders in the Black community and the academy hinges upon respectability. Many of them grew up during a time where everything they did had to meet the approval and standard of whiteness. This burden was so engrained into every fiber of their existence that they now use it to measure later generations and socially crucify those who refuse to submit to it. This burden was a burden that was far too great for them to carry, and it is even more egregious for them to pass it on. Yet here we are at a crossroads where we must decide that in order to completely liberate ourselves from the glaring gaze of whiteness, we must give ourselves permission to reject it. To reject the hold that it has had on our ancestors and the hold that our elders are trying to place on us. Millennials and Generation Z are clear in that we refuse to relinquish our power, our fight, and our liberation. We will use our voices and raise our fists even when they both shake. Fighting the power does not mean that we are not concerned but it means that we choose fighting for our liberation over folding ourselves into oppressive systems.

Music as Resistance

Many people believe that those who fought for liberation and led our most successful movements were not afraid. I am certain that there is a level of fear that exists within anyone who uses their body to fight for freedom. However, it is better to be afraid than to be silent and allowing yourself to be reduced to less than your own humanity. People ask me how do I speak in front of crowds of people and I always explain to them that I still experience nervousness. The difference is I do not allow my nerves to take hold and cause me to rethink or second guess my purpose. There is power in your fear because it means that you care and that you are moving with a moral code unfamiliar to our oppressors. One of the ways that our ancestors would navigate their fears was through songs and hymns of praise as a means of calming the soul and also their nerves, I am sure. Being liberated is also an important facet of our [Black] music (Mcclendon 1976). As Mcclendon (1976) states, Black culture, and our understanding of it have grown from coping with social constraints placed upon us. How we have managed to deal with these constraints has impacted us in different ways. Some of us choose to avoid as a means of not shaking any trees and others of us want to rip the tree up from the roots. How you decide to view either of these reactions is up to you, but one fact remains and that is if we all choose avoidance, who will liberate us? Who will save us? Who will protect us? Resistance and liberation along with fighting back are our only recourse. *Fight the power* requires for us to do exactly that.

The only way to liberation is through our oppressors and not by asking them. Through liberatory music we can draw on the experiences of our ancestors who through song, resisted. Despite the attempt of enslavers to disconnect our people from all aspects of our culture, the enslaved Africans found ways to appropriate and transpose what white people gave them (Ladson-Billings 2015). The enslaved used these tools to create a new religion, a form of resistance, and they did it through music (Ladson-Billings 2015). Music for us was never just about music. It is always about telling stories of not just our struggles but also highlighting our strength and reminding others of where we are going and how far we have come. Music for Black folks has always been liberatory! Our music has always had dual meanings that were only to be interpreted for and by us (Ladson-Billings 2015). When I thought about what I wanted this book to be about I wanted it similar to our music to have a dual meaning for us. I wanted Black millennials to see themselves through these words and I wanted them to relate to or find comfort in the name of each of the chapters which are named after liberation songs. Songs that might be familiar to many of us and songs that we might be less acquainted with. Consider each of the chapters of this book as a soundtrack for liberation. Make it a playlist and read this book simultaneously. Allow it to help you to consider and think about what your role in all of this is. How do you see your strengths and skills as an asset as we *fight the power*? Each of us like a song or band must play an integral part in freeing us. One missing piece makes the song, the band, or the fight impossible, and that is the perspective that we must always have. We each have a role.

When we think back during the time of our grandparents and great-grandparents, we saw both elders and youth participating in the fight for Civil Rights. Through fear, threats, and incarceration they fought back against Jim Crow and the administration that allowed for it (Litwack 2009). Children like Ruby Bridges and the Little Rock Nine had to dodge spitting and mobs of angry white parents and adults simply because they dared to learn (Litwack 2009). When we think about every aspect of our existence in this country, we have always been troubled by white people unwilling to let us know any aspect of peace. The same white people who clutch their pearls, their purses, and lock their doors if you happen to cross paths with them. The same white people who hide their daughters because they see Black men as a danger to their virtue and purity. White people have consistently shown themselves to us as attackers of our freedom and our bodies, yet they are the ones who live their everyday lives in constant fear of or obsessed with Black people. If their obsession with our existence was not deadly, I might be able to find the humor in it. Whiteness disallows for them to even see the humanity in our children while fighting illegally to protect their own. If that is not enough to make you want to knock shyt over, nothing will! White children are not more worthy of protection than Black children. White children are not more deserving of educational access than Black children. White children are not more deserving of peace and quiet in their everyday existence than Black children, and if you disagree even slightly you are the problem.

INTERNALIZING THE POISON OF ANTI-BLACKNESS

How old were you when you decided that you hated what you looked like? For me, I was about 11-years old and in the sixth grade. Puberty was beginning in my body, and I was not old enough to realize what was happening. I stepped into my husky jeans era and my older brother was still slim. I remained the more solid of the two of us throughout middle school and girls noticed it. I remember all of the girls in our peer group who loved my older brother who was always a handsome fella. I did not have what I considered to be the most favorable of the features offered to my siblings and I via the gene pool lottery. I was darker in complexion than my siblings who lived with me and I was also the one who experienced violence by close family friends as a result of it. I remember there were times during that period of my life where I refused to even look in the mirror. I would critique my features, the shape of my head, my full lips, and the mole that is smacked square in the middle of my forehead. I began to see the things within myself that my former babysitters thought made me undeserving when compared to my siblings. I think if I am honest about that time period with myself, I would say that I hated myself. I never thought to harm myself and it is still not something that I can fathom but it was a time in my life where I dealt with a profound sadness that no amount of forced joy could heal. The anti-Blackness that was thrust upon me in my developmental years were resurfacing and it was during a transitional period in my physical body.

As a society we spend more time focused on what to say to our young girls as that transition takes hold, but most boys only receive the *birds and the bee's* discussion. No one thinks it appropriate to tell boys about what is happening to our bodies and we all kind of just let it happen. By the time I was in eighth grade and an athlete I had a growth spurt and dropped quite a bit of weight. It was enough weight to be noticeable and a staff member in a scholar program that I was part of pulled me aside to discuss it with me. She mentioned that there was some concern about my weight loss and asked if I were eating regularly. I never told my mother this and she will read this and find out with the rest of the world, but it was real, and it happened. I can laugh about it now because if you asked my mom who had three children entering puberty at the same time, we ate everything in sight! That time period was really difficult for me but as I moved onto high school, I began to have a different view of myself, a more positive one. We do not often talk about the impact that anti-Blackness can have on the development of Black people from childhood through adulthood. Most of the issues that many of us dealt with in our development can be directly linked to anti-Blackness, anti-Black racism, and white supremacy. Having the frame of thought and the words to name my experiences has helped me to be able to resolve myself of some of the harm associated with them.

Anti-Blackness is found on every continent of the world that colonization touched (Howard and Sommers 2015). Essentially anywhere that whiteness was allowed to create a racialized hierarchy anti-Blackness will thrive. One of the most disingenuous things that ever occurred was spurring the lie that as a result of President Obama's election that the United States had become post-racial. We are no further from racism than we were when stolen Africans arrived on this land, it just looks different. The belief that anti-Black racism is a thing of the past while also indicating that a white vigilante killing a Black child in Washington, D.C. was the neighborly thing to do is a gaslight of gross proportions. Critical consciousness which is also known as sociopolitical development or conscientization is an intervention aimed at preventing, mitigating, and resisting racialized trauma (Mosley, et al. 2021). A behavioral component of *critical consciousness* is *critical action* and individuals who engage in *critical action* are seen or known as *activists* (Mosley, et al. 2021). Liberation work and activist work require that each of us be aware of racism both overt and covert and self-aware of anti-Blackness and how it causes us to view each other. Being conscious means that you operate in a space of knowing and with pure intention for the liberation of not just yourself but the liberation of all of us born into the struggle against our will. Being critically aware of how anti-Blackness harms Black people helps you to operate in a way that is healing for Black people (Mosley, et al. 2021). Part of our liberatory work includes us also telling the truth about how we participate in anti-Blackness at times unknowingly but regardless of intent it is still harmful and the work of white supremacy.

The politics of respectability allowed for us to believe that Rosa Parks was the first Black woman to refuse to give up her seat in the face of anti-Black racism. True historical storytelling makes us aware that the first known person to be arrested for refusing to give up her seat was actually a pregnant, unwed, and dark-skinned teenager just fifteen years of age named, Claudette Colvin (Leath and Mims 2021). Parks was made the face of the movement not because she was anymore of a heroine than Colvin was. She was made the heroine because she had a "look," and that look was respectable. Parks was fair-skinned, middle class, and she was a graduate of a private high school (Leath and Mims 2021) which made her more worthy of defense and protection, a perspective rooted in internalized anti-Blackness and respectability. As educated as our movement leaders were they were still exhibiting and upholding aspects of white supremacy that made them believe that women were not to be upfront or anything other than conservative and conventional. White supremacy does not need our help and it was that time period that keeps Black respectability alive today.

Anti-Blackness is our Achilles' heel!

We say that we hate white supremacy, and we hate that white people will not leave us alone, so why do we repeat their behaviors? I like to give some level of grace for our people in how they are often upholders of white supremacist concepts. However, I have personally exchanged unpleasantries with relatives who even after being made aware of the anti-Blackness of their statements continued to double down. One of my favorite aunties likes to use the f-word and I have often told her that she needed to find another word to describe her feelings of her queer male neighbor. She mentioned the slur several times to me and each time I asked her to not do it and she argued that she was the adult and that I do not control what she says out of her mouth. I simply ended the call and have sense refused to take her calls. She also will find this out as she reads this. We can only claim ignorance to things that we do when we are unaware of their roots. However, that same perspective cannot stand up as a defense when someone lovingly made you aware of your anti-Blackness. My aunt is not alone in her beliefs and absolutely makes concessions for other things that she considers acceptable sins. Is it hypocritical? Absolutely. As a personal choice and an act of resistance I refuse to deal with anyone who chooses to operate in any way that is deemed anti-Black and harmful. One thing about the generations that precede us is that they are not always open to learning from millennials and regardless of our expertise and experience they will, based upon some nonsense biblical assertion, believe that they should be respected in spite of. In spite of the harm that anti-Black racism caused them. In spite of the harm that internalized anti-Blackness caused them. In spite of the harm that colorism caused them. In spite of the harm that respectability caused them. Knowing full well how much they disagreed with it and hated it being impressed upon them, they still do it to us.

For this I will always stop them dead in their tracks and ask them simply, why? Why do you continue to settle in your ways that have harmed your people? Why do you continue to be a representative of something you espouse that you hate? Why do you see our resistance as a negative thing and instead of an inevitable good? I ask these questions and most of them do not have adequate responses and the reality is that the harm of anti-Black racism has made them this way. Hardened and at times harmful. For Black women, politics of respectability are deeply tied to controlling images of Black womanhood (Leath and Mims 2021). When I think of the ways that Black women police and subjugate other Black women through the guise of respectable womanhood, I am immediately reminded of Patricia Hill Collins and her *matrix of domination.* Most recently I saw a tweet from a lame Philadelphia rapper in reference to Lori Harvey's dating patterns. He made a comment that said something like "*y'all let that gal f#%k anybody,*" and I immediately felt rage. I was enraged because I began to think how could someone who had to win his freedom from the state not be aware of the role of white supremacy in the context of body control. The idea that a young woman cannot or should not have the freedom to date at her own liberty without judgement or rumors has never settled well in my spirit. We do not police a man regardless of how many people he sleeps with so long as his sexual appetite is cis-heterosexual, and I have a problem with that.

My liberation praxis does not allow me to view patriarchy as liberation or an inevitable good in any way that it is packaged. *Fight the power* to me means going toe-to-toe with anything that hinges upon the liberation and the freedom of any of my people, even if that enemy is patriarchal heterosexism. These hands are rated e-for everyone. Images of control refer to stereotypical images of Black women that are used by individuals in society [*usually white people but not always*] to rationalize how they oppress Black women through sexual, sociopolitical, and economic means (Leath and Mims 2021). The idea that Lori Harvey needs an NDA is proof that our people also have an issue with how we measure our loyalty and relationship to Black women and their body autonomy. The idea that a Black woman can pick up men and put them down with the ease of disregarding a bad drink seems preposterous to most and that reason is because many do not view Black woman as capable people. If that is your perspective, it says a great deal more about you than it ever will about Black women. I just want to know if when white people give out agents of white supremacy badges are you first or last in line? Do they allow you in the front door to get your badge, or do you still have to enter through the back door or on designated days?

The treatment of Lori, Jada, and Megan to name a few is directly related to the *Jezebel stereotype.* It allows for people to police their sexuality and label them more promiscuous than other racialized groups even though the term stems from the period of enslavement when the enslaved were often raped (Leath and Mims 2021). My aggravation with my brothas and sistas who carry on this trope is that at a bare minimum we all understand that oversexualizing Black women has roots in slavery. Since we are all aware of this ideology, I believe choosing to further perpetuate this harm means that you have chosen your side in our fight for liberation. The side that you chose is not the side of liberation but a side of continuation, and that continuation is that of anti-Black racism and white supremacy. The same ideologies that say that single Black women cannot date until their heart is content is the same one that makes you all ask single Black women when they plan to marry and where are their children. This perspective is related to how Black women and women in general are socialized as a result of patriarchy and heterosexism (Leath and Mims 2021). Black girls and women are forced into comporting themselves into the acceptance of dominant gender-based norms like childrearing and marriage (Leath and Mims 2021). The idea that some women have never wanted to mother primarily because they witnessed what their foremothers endured is unconscionable for some. As for me and my house, I fully understand. Having your dreams placed on hold because of a husband and children is not desirable to all Black women and it is essential that we respect that if we truly believe in liberation. Marriage is not the goal for everyone nor is birthing or rearing children and everyone needs to release themselves from the Eurocentric belief that it is. If you want to be married, get married. And leave everyone else alone. Black families are supposed to be teaching Black girls and young women about misogynoir and the harm of it, but the teaching should not come because your family is replicating it.

In our context for understanding why we say Black Lives Matter it must be understood that this stance is a queer politic (Greene-Hayes and James 2017). Not queer in a sense of sexuality although the founders are members of the LGBTQ+ community. I mean queer in that stating and asserting that Black Lives Matter is meant to push up against the status quo that tells us incessantly that they [*Black lives*] do not. In my interrogation and other scholars' interrogation of previous liberatory movements we understand that there was a great deal accomplished while holding space for critiquing the parts of those movements that were anti-Black and wrong (Greene-Hayes and James 2017). Most of the previous iterations of exercises in liberation did not do a service to women or queer people who were ostensibly present and intentionally excluded. Had it not been for Mahalia Jackson we might have never heard of Dr. Martin Luther King Jr's dream. Had it not been for Bayard Rustin we might not have ever known how to navigate interstate racism nor would the famous "*I have a Dream*" speech had a place to occur.

Jackson is a woman and Rustin was a gay man. Both of which are often dismissed from the larger conversation regarding their roles in those early Civil Rights movements. One of the things that we understand about anti-Blackness and the socially constructed rendering of Black bodies as inhuman, inherently problematic, and disposable endures in the cultural ethos of both American social institutions and some aspects of the patriarchal Black politic (Warren and Coles 2020). Among our Black men there exists this strange dynamic where we battle between wanting liberation and wanting to be like the white men who oppress us. I believe there exists some core belief that what white people and especially white men do is bad but mainly because they are *white* and not because they are *oppressive*. What I cannot seem to grasp is the concept that some of my brothas carry wherein they are willing to play the role of oppressor so long as they are not who is being oppressed. Many of them would scoff at this assertion but how else do you address their attitudes toward single Black [attractive] women, queer men, and women, trans persons, larger bodies, and the idea that each of the aforementioned must be controlled and or silenced? These are not the beliefs and values of someone who truly has a Black politic rooted in full liberation inclusive of every Black person and not just the ones they prefer.

LIBERATION FOR ALL OR NO LIBERATION FOR THEE!

One of my favorite quotes from Freire (1970) states, in the oppressed person's desire to regain their humanity they must not become in turn oppressors, but rather restorers of humanity. I recite this to my students often when teaching about social differentiation and inequality or any discussion surrounding racialized hierarchical structures. I recite this for my students so that they understand the work in disruption and ultimately liberation is never to swap places with your oppressor. It is instead to create a society where there is no desire to oppress or ability to do so. A society where everyone lives as they are, and how they see themselves, without fear or judgement of a majority ruling class. A society where people are inevitably good because there exists no need to lie, cheat, or steal. This world seems unfathomable because we have only known a world where the bad actor was the ruling class and any idea of good is cast off as a handout to the undeserving therefore unacceptable. *Fighting the power* requires us to think outside of what we know as norms and to push back against any idea that seeks to create and uphold societal differences between *the haves* and *the have-nots*.

Black women are the most self-less beings that God ever created, and it is not even close. Black women will go to war for any and everybody while never receiving the same collective support at large. This self-less disposition is because Black women have long recognized the special circumstances of their lives within the context of this social experiment that is America (King 1988). The commonalities that Black women share with all women while also accounting for the very unique differences that make them Black women and connect them to us, Black men (King 1988). The duality of systemic inequity like racism and sexism remain pervasive for Black women further compounded by class differences and distinctions (King 1988). The constant comparison to sexism and racism as compatible is a discrepancy that white women cannot seem to fathom. In a recent in class discussion a white female student mentioned how being a woman was comparable to racism, and a Black female student chimed in and said I am Black, and I am a woman. This same argument is one that white women like Elizabeth Cady Stanton have made since the 1860s (King 1988). They simply do not understand the difference and it is why many liberal white women who hate patriarchy are still racist. Race is not comparable to sex, and it is set apart in the oppression hierarchy. A Black woman could never use her Blackness to elevate herself above a white woman using solely her race. Whereas a white woman can always use her race to elevate herself above the standing of Black women. White women seem to conveniently forget about the *invisible* privilege that accompanies their race category while clamoring over being mistreated by the men they birth, raise, and refuse to hold accountable. White women want liberation for them but not for anyone else, and that is a racism problem. In conversations with non-Black women researchers, they often hypothesize that Black women should choose only one of their minoritized categories to cling to and the suggestion is almost always the class category (King 1988). According to King (1988), this is because the fix for many small-minded people is to simply provide economic support or advice as a means of eliminating this stressor. Often not realizing that wealth does not exclude Black women from racism and sexism [see: Jada, both Megan's, and Lori, again]. Black women have always been forced to exist within the margins and taught to play small when doing so. Black women have to contend with white women, white men, and also Black men who all often view Black women as a threat. Imagine having to fight for your right to exist in your body all day and then having to come home to raise a family and do battle with your partner over dominance.

Millennial and Gen Z women are decidedly clear about their desire to not be like some of our mothers, grandmothers, and great-grandmothers and are choosing themselves. A move I wholeheartedly support! I think about the women who exist in my life whether they be friends from childhood, college, or graduate school years, I often think of them when I decide to show up in the world. I also think of the women in my family. My mother, grandmother, and great-grandmothers whom I have had the pleasure of sharing earth and breath with. I also think of my othermothers like my godmother and the women who have showed up for me in motherly ways [my aunties]. Understanding that each and every one of these women has her own unique as well as shared experiences with other Black women in this country which are coupled consistently with racism, sexism, and class struggles. For these reasons, I am and will always be an intersectional feminist. How could I not be? More importantly, how could you not be? Understanding the nuances of Blackness is one thing. Understanding the nuances of Blackness through the lens of a woman will forever change you. *Liberation for us, not just for me!*

RESISTANCE BEGETS PERSISTENCE

One of the greatest lessons to learn in this life is that through your resistance you will find a way to persist. When we think back to the comment that the famous rapper made about the enslaved choosing to remain in their bondage, I am reminded of what it took. I am reminded that had they not persisted none of us would be here. Being mindful that resistance looks different for many of us just as joy and rest are both forms of resistance that show up in different ways. Our ancestors resisted by not giving up! They resisted by keeping parts of Africa with them so that they could pass it down to us. Disregarding some of the genetic gifts that they gave us is an act of anti-Blackness within itself. African Americans familial dynamic where we are largely connected by space as well as time is a very African practice. The concept of *othermothers* and *otherfathers* is also African because of the way that families both by blood and marriage would reside together and collectively rare the children.

It takes a village was not a lie and was a regular practice. Look within some of your own families if/when an elder stepped in to take on the rearing of a relative that they did not birth. The belief is that the child is the responsibility of the family collective and if you are in a better condition to rare or support the child then you do so. Understanding that choosing not to name our children watered down Eurocentric names is also an act of rebellion and resistance. We are told as an aspect of respectability that we should name our children certain ways and to always appear certain ways and baby, that is that white people shyt! They told you not to wear your hair in braids and then they go to Cancun and return with braids. They tell you that your clothing is inappropriately fitted and then they go and get body work done to look more like you. We are spinning our heels in the sand desperately attempting to assimilate and as many of us run away from our inherited Blackness they are attempting to monetize it.

Black women will make a TikTok sharing beauty and hair secrets intended for other Black women and a white woman will steal the idea, which was never intended for her, and cause entire businesses to water down their products for their use. White women have always understood that a Black woman's survival hinges upon her ability to tap into all of the cultural, economic, and social resources available to her from the dominant culture as well as her own culture (King 1988). This understanding is precisely why white women stealing from Black women is much more egregious than most can conceptualize. White women have stolen from Black women since the period of enslavement when they would force enslaved Black women to prioritize feeding their white children over the enslaved woman's own child. They have never cared about the burdens that they place on and at the feet of Black women which is why erasure is something that they take zero issue in participating in. Liberal white women must understand that being liberal is simply not enough. Ask yourself, what are you willing to give up? How much are you willing to lose to liberate Black women and Black people? Your participation in the liberatory movement is more than simply walking beside us and claiming to be an anti-racist. It is demanding of you to be willing to take a loss and understand and support that such a loss is intended for the betterment of society.

Understanding our need to resist which allows us to persist takes us to the acknowledgment of the need for Black placemaking. Placemaking allows for Black people not to ignore external assaults like police brutality and gentrification, nor does it allow them to ignore internal dangers like harassment, homophobia, and homicide (Hunter, et al. 2016). Black placemaking refers to the ability that Black residents have to change oppressive aspects of where they live into places of celebration, politics, pleasure, and play (Hunter et al. 2016). The ability to shift how we experience where we live is a form of resistance innately connected to our sense of belonging and community building free of oppressive ideologies. As was true in Africa, we never needed paternalistic whiteness telling us how to walk, talk, and or chew gum. White people convinced themselves that we needed them and their permission. The rejection of white acceptance is considered radical because many of us cannot imagine a world where white people do not control all aspects of our humanity. Understanding who you are and why *fighting the power* is essential to that learning will move you further away from white acceptance and closer to self-actualization. We do not need or require their permission to live a life of abundance and although that should not be a radical act, it is.

I WOULD RATHER BE . . . RADICAL

The day that I made peace with the spirit that resides within me was the day that I accepted my purpose in the disruption. Since I was a child, I have always had an unsettled spirit when I believe that people were being wronged. I can remember growing up in Utica and living on West Street on what we called the parkway. I was no older than about ten years of age at a maximum. My older brother who you have heard a lot about, and a childhood friend of ours lived across the street from us. One day after a nap [*yes, I have always believed in rest*], I came outside and noticed that my brother and our friend were not in any of the usual places which were typically our porch or his parents' porch. I look across the street and there was Tony who was the bully of the block at that time [*the bullies took turns during different seasons, I guess*] and he was using a belt to hit my brother and our childhood friend. Without a second thought, I hightailed it across the street and beat his ass. I am talking full on blows to that hard ass head of his. I was afraid of Tony as well but not too afraid to throw hands if and when it was necessary. I did not and do not play about my loved ones as Tony would learn on that day. That was not the only instance where I took up for a relative or sibling of mine. Although a middle child, there were several times where I absolutely operated like the oldest and it was usually when it was time to get busy. My brother during that time was a lot more patient than I was and my sister never had to get her hands dirty, I was known to handle it. I guess you could say that resistance regardless of who the opposition was, was something that was born within me.

When we hear people and more particularly white people discuss Black radicals like Dr. Martin Luther King Jr., they always discuss him juxtaposed to Malcolm X. Why? Because they like to paint the picture of Dr. King as this passive Black man and one that we should all as Black people strive to be like. They seldom mention that Dr. King was sick of them too! Malcolm had a no-nonsense perspective and believed in the uplifting of Blackness free from the white gaze or the white permission slip. Since they could not control Malcolm and the strength of his voice much like the Black Panther party, they sought to tarnish their images and paint them as violent. Who in this country has been more violent than white people? *Answer: Not a soul.* White people would kill, rape, and steal before you could bat an eye but somehow, they remain the progenitors of moral high ground. A joke.

I would rather be radical because being a radical is necessary to bring about true non-performative social change (Fitzgerald 2014). Radicals are the people often looked at in a negative way because non-radicals believe that you are causing trouble. Those people are absolutely right! In the words of the late and great John Lewis, I am committed to getting into *good trouble!* Nothing in this social experiment has ever been given to the colonized without demanding it. We asked to be able to assimilate and white people said, no! We asked them to leave us alone and white people said, no! It is beyond time for the polite asking to cease and it is time that we start demanding that we be left alone, and we be given what rightfully belongs to us. The political elite always seem to have our phone numbers when they need our help in stopping the extremists from sending us into a dictatorship, and it is beyond time for them to return the favor. We do not need brass statues of the people that racism turned into martyrs. What we need are *reparations* and to see the end of white supremacy and anti-Black racism in our lifetime. Anything else outside of that is performative and a liberal attempt to pacify us. Keep your offensive methods of pacification and give us our liberation and give us what we are owed. I would much rather be seen as radical as I *fight the power* than to ever be seen as someone who accepted whiteness as the end all be all.

REFERENCES

Fitzgerald, Andy. 2014. *Being labeled a 'radical' is meant to be an insult. History tells us otherwise.* January 20. https://www.theguardian.com/commentisfree/2014/jan/20/we-need-radicals-for-social-change.

Freire, Paulo. 1970. *Pedagogy of the oppressed.* New York: The Continuum International Publishing Group Inc.

Greene-Hayes, Ahmad, and Joy James. 2017. "Cracking the Codes of Black Power Struggles:Hacking, Hacked,and BlackLives Matter." *The Black Scholar: Journal of Black Studies and Research, 47:3* 68–78.

Howard, Simin, and Samuel Sommers. 2015. "Exploring the Enigmatic Link Between Religion and Anti-Black Attitudes." *Social and Personality Psychology Compass 9/9* 495–510.

Hunter, Marcus Anthony, Mary Patillo, Zandria F. Robinson, and Keeanga-Yamahtta Taylor. 2016. "Black Placemaking: Celebration, Play, and Poetry." *Theory, Culture, & Society, 0(0)* 1–26.

King, Deborah K. 1988. "Multiple Jeopardy, Multiple Consciousness: The Context of a Black Feminist Ideology." *Signs, Vol. 14. No.1* 42–72.

Ladson-Billings, Gloria. 2015. "Chapter 25: You Gotta Fight the Power: The Place of Music in Social Justice Education." In *The Oxford Handbook of Social Justice in Music Education*, by Cathy Benedict, Patrick Scmidt, Gary Spruce and Paul Woodford, 407–420. Oxford University Press.

Leath, Seanna, and Lauren Mims. 2021. "A qualitative exploration of Black women's familial socialization on controlling images of Black womanhood and the internalization of respectability politics." *Journal of Family Studies* 1–18.

Litwack, Leon F. 2009. "'Fight The Power!' The Legacy of the Civil Rights Movement." *The Journal of Southern History, 75(1)* 3–28.

Mcclendon, William H. 1976. "Black Music: Sound and Feeling for Black Liberation." *The Black Scholar: Journal of Black Studies and Research, 7(5)* 20–25.

Mosley, Della, Candace Hargons, Carolyn Meiller, Blanka Angyal, Paris Wheeler, Candice Davis, and Danelle Stevens-Watkins. 2021. "Critical Consciousness of Anti-Black Racism: A Practical Model to Prevent and Resist Racial Trauma." *Journal of Counseling Psychology Vol 68. No.1* 1–16.

Warren, Chezare, and Justin Coles. 2020. "Trading Spaces: Antiblackness and Reflections on Black Education Futures." *Equity & Excellence in Education Vol 53. No.3* 382–398.

Chapter 5

R.E.S.P.E.C.T

Current Debates Around Bailey's Misogynoir

WORD TO AUNTIE RERE!

Aretha Franklin's ballad about respect talks about being a Black woman and needing to be respected by the man in her life. This song can be used as an anthem for the liberation of Black women. As the most consistently disrespected marginalized group within and outside of Black culture it is imperative that this chapter addresses this harm. Politics of respectability which are rooted in controlling those that they are imposed upon are often used to subjugate Black women. This can show up in arguments about whether or not hair bonnets which are used to protect Black hair can or should be worn in public. The agents of respectability see it as a stain on the appearance of Blackness. However, what should be considered is how this thought process often acts as an agent of white supremacy. The attack on Nikole Hannah-Jones and what she endured at UNC Chapel Hill in regard to her tenure battle applies here as well. White America has been enraged with her since the launch of the *1619 project* and at every turn try to discredit her. The attack on Hannah-Jones is more widespread because she is a Black woman. This chapter will interweave Dr. Moya Bailey's *misogynoir* as a way to highlight the way that anti-black racism affects Black women.

Black women constantly find themselves on the short end of the stick in regard to liberation. They often find themselves their only advocates, protectors, and allies. The media and the world constantly remind Black women of how disposable they perceive them to be. Whether it be the hundreds of missing Black girls or ESPN's Rachel Nichols unwarranted attack on Maria Taylor, simply because. Black women find themselves on the defense within their own community when they are attacked by other Black women and

Black men alike. While also coping with societal attacks by whiteness at every turn in every way. Black women are worthy of protection and respect and that is one of the key targets of true Black liberation. Most Americans like to pretend that the enslavement of Africans in this country was so long ago. Many of them fail to realize that there are African Americans and white people who are living today who shared the earth with enslaved people or their children. One of the greatest personal rebrands in this social experiment has absolutely been white women. At least with white men they have been consistent with who they are and what is important to them. White women have most people distracted by focusing on their disdain for patriarchy not realizing that white women are the key to the success of racism, white supremacy, and subsequently patriarchy.

UC Berkeley Associate Professor of History, Dr. Stephanie Jones-Rogers told us in great detail about the ills of white women during the antebellum south in her award-winning book, *They Were Her Property*. Her truth telling of the role of white women during the period of enslavement helped me to understand their relationship with their societal position, disdain for the unearned position of white men, and hatred and envy of the women whom they enslaved. We [*society*] often discuss the role of white men during that time period and white women largely escaped ridicule by delving into faux feminist endeavors of liberation. My reference to their feminism as faux is because it was not inclusive of all women and most assuredly did not include the enslaved, the poor, or the disabled. White liberatory movements were never inclusive of the people native to this land or those enslaved to it so it should always be critiqued with that understanding in mind.

During the period of enslavement wet nursing was rampant and it was a very unique way of exploiting enslaved African women (West and Knight 2017). Feeding another woman's child was considered a form of labor but it was only a labor that a lactating woman who had borne her own children could produce (West and Knight 2017). This very unique bond was used to manipulate the motherhood of enslaved women by their enslavers [*usually white women*] to no end (West and Knight 2017). This phenomenon helps to understand the inextricable connection between enslaved African women and white women throughout history. White women have always viewed African American women as sublevel to their own womanhood and they mince no words in their objection to equity between the two. Enslaved African women had deep ties to the white children whom they nursed and who would then grow up and become the enslavers of the women who nursed them. Black women are often viewed as the nurses and caretakers of society. Fast forward to the politic of America and Black women of today and how this country nurses at the bosom of Black women politic, only to turn away from them the moment the deed is done. America to African American women is like the white child to the enslaved African woman. They are needed when the defenseless country or child call to them and then immediately dismissed and disregarded. Black women have nursed this country constantly and their reward for their selflessness has always been disrespect. How do you rationalize this behavior by any other definition than *misogynoir*. This experience is only an experience that enslaved African women and African American women of today share in. The gift of whiteness has long allowed for the degradation of enslaved people and namely African women and disallowed for white people to ever be held accountable for it. The era of social media and smart phones has allowed for the first time ever the possibility for white accountability.

KAREN AS A RECKONING

At this point I have no idea who the first person was to dub the behavior of white women behaving badly via social media as *Karen*-behavior. What I do know is that for the first time aside from the footage of the white women taunting Black people during the Civil Rights era, we have proof of white women not pretending to be docile. Personally, I detest the term *Karen* because it like everything else gives white women cover for their dirty deeds. The only thing that I can appreciate about the nickname and subsequent recording is that it allows for the elite investigators of Black and liberal Twitter to come together to properly identify racist white women. I am reminded of how many enslaved Africans and African Americans have lost their lives because a white woman lied. Whether it be children like Emmett Till, or George Stinney who were both a mere aged fourteen when they were murdered or whole towns and cities like Tulsa and Rosewood being torched behind a lie. I find it interesting that white women have been made out to be damsels in distress when understanding the real history of this country will inform you that they were just as bad as their white male counterparts, maybe even the fuel of it all. 55 percent of white women voted for Trump in spite of all that he had said and done regarding their fellow women. What the 55 percent repeatedly showed us is that they will always choose their whiteness over what is morally right because they understand that at the end of the day, they will still reap the benefits of their racialized category.

There is something very profound about a people who on one hand adamantly oppose being oppressed while staunchly supporting the oppression of others. I believe *audacious* is the word that I used in another chapter to describe their behavior and ethical framing. White women at large were never bothered by the oppression of the enslaved they just wanted the right to have equal say in the discourse as I mentioned before. Many of them have cried about being called Karen and have said that they have considered changing their names to avoid ridicule and the like. Please be clear that if you have ever fallen out about the name Karen and felt personally attacked by it that you are certifiably not an anti-racist. True anti-racist *Karen*'s would absolutely understand that part of what they need to give up in this fight for liberation is being sensitive about being named, *Karen*. Imagine being able to live in the world where the most degrading thing that society calls you is Karen and that name being the single thing that makes you feel attacked. *Karen, please!* I have never once heard a true co-conspirator named Karen burst into tears because of her name or make the argument for why she needed to change it. The summer of 2020 showed us another version of the Karen. The version where her tears became the focal point of discussion during the summer of the widespread BLM movements. Countless white women began randomly texting their "few" Black friends to ask what they could do and to offer their support for the "difficult" times as if racism just appeared in 2020. It as usual is gut wrenching the way that white people will always find a way to center themselves in *ANY* discourse regarding white supremacy and racism. Which is in fact a version of white supremacy and racism, go figure.

I am often caught off guard when white women cry in front of me over racism. What is their expectation of me and their expectation of us? What it should not be is an ask of comfort because the comfort in those moments does not belong with or to them. *Tighten up!* My annoyance with the tears is because they are intentional to disarm our justified rage. Often times, white individuals use their power and privilege to ensure that Black folks conform to their white notions of civility by threat of violence or death (Williams 2020). According to Williams (2020), white women use a particular type of social control through surveillance, policing, and patrolling of Black people in public spaces to uphold white supremacist ideologies of law and order. Which is interesting because they have zero concern for you or a Black child's well-being as they commit such heinous acts of racism, but the minute they see a camera cue the water works. White women have a crafty way of making themselves the victim particularly in instances when they are deadass wrong. As the result of being racialized as white and whiteness having the value of property the behavior of the white person as the police in public space seems for them appropriate (Williams 2020). White people who have not done the work in understanding why their behavior is an inevitable harm to everyone will be offended by any assertion of the sort. What I can tell you is that I, and other critical scholars of race have no reason to benefit from telling lies about whiteness or its beneficiaries. Whether you choose to acknowledge the truth of our research or accounts is a personal matter of your own, but I can assure you that it will not stop us from telling the truth. Throughout history from antebellum slavery to Jim Crow and the Civil Rights movement white people have always sough to control space and disallow Black existing even when it caused no harm (Williams 2020). One of the things that has always been very unique about whiteness is that as much as it wants to be a separatist, it is not as effective in white only spaces. In order for whiteness to be maximized and raised in status there must be marginalized people present.

BLACK WOMEN AS BOSSES AND
WHITE PEOPLE AS EMPLOYEES

I follow Dr. Monica Cox on Twitter and have for quite some time. Dr. Cox is a Distinguished Professor of Engineering at The Ohio State University. I reference Dr. Cox because she is a Black woman in leadership who I have had the privilege of watching her share her experiences as a leader and the trauma associated with it. Dr. Cox is obviously not the only Black woman to share in this experience but there is something here that is worth discussing. Historically, the academy was created for the education of white men and the idea of white women entering the space was unfathomable let alone a Black woman. In 1878, Ohio State University graduated its first class which was comprised of six white men (Stouffer-Lerch 2020). After some protests Ohio State graduated a white woman one-year later (Stouffer-Lerch 2020). The first African American to graduate from Ohio State would graduate about a decade later but that did not change the atmosphere for African American students (Stouffer-Lerch 2020). Students who attended the university during the 1940s and 1950s discussed that the curriculum was both Eurocentric and culturally insensitive and students had no recourse (Stouffer-Lerch 2020). According to Stouffer-Lerch (2020), African American students were not allowed to reside on campus until the 1950s which only further affirms that the culture of the institution was rooted in anti-Black racism. PWIs and their attitudes toward white separatism in the pre-Civil Rights era has not changed much even with their bustling enrollments of students of color. The campus climate surveys that are never made public hide the truth of the African American experience of all campus stakeholders. Knowing the history of The Ohio State University and white campuses which share its make-up across the country, there is no wonder that successful Black women like Dr. Cox are experiencing misogynoir. The roots of hate in majority white spaces are buried so deep that no amount of performative measures of DEI can contain them.

Black women exists in the dominant white patriarchal context of the American social experiment and are often not considered welcomed or allowed to belong in academia (Johnson 2022). Black women are often forced out of academia because their mere existence in the space is enough to make white people inferior. Regardless of how small Black women are taught to play or how friendly they come across there will always be white resistance to their presence as an exhibition used for the establishment of white dominance. Knowing this about the white reception to Black women provides an opportunity for us to question why white people are not expected to be "professional." Only we are coached into how we should behave around white people. How we should speak; how we should hold our forks; how we should dress, all for the sake of being seen as respectable. I highly doubt that white people are trained from their parents on how to act professional and appropriate when they are in the presence of Blackness whether it be considered excellent or not. Regardless of these experiences with whiteness Black women still achieve at statistically higher levels. Imagine what would be possible for Black women in America and the world if misogynoir was not an expected aspect of their lived experience. Black women anger white men because they are the antithesis of upper-middle class, cis-heteropatriarchal, manhood in a society built on capitalism (Johnson 2022). The old adage of *if you cannot beat them, join them* does not work for white men in regard to Black women. Instead, if they cannot beat them, they bully, defame, and minimize them as a measure of their manhood. As Johnson (2022) states, Black women are often undermined and questioned about this expertise in an attempt to discredit them and make them second guess themselves. Who wants to live their lives in this manner? *Answer: It is certainly NOT Black women!*

Imagine having your entire existence consistently undermined, cut down, and made a mockery of all for shyts and giggles. Many white women will say *it happens to us all the time!* Exactly! If this is also you experience, would it not make sense that when you are presented with the opportunity to do something about, you do it? Your fight for liberation cannot be rooted in being equally oppressive. It must be rooted in eliminating any opportunity for systemic inequality to exist for anyone. Grown ass Black women find themselves being chided by white women and men anytime they feel like it regardless of the age of Black women. We witnessed this in 2017 when Congresswoman Maxine Waters and journalist April Ryan were belittled by Bill O'Reilly and then Press Secretary Sean Spicer because of their hair and having the ability to shake their head in disagreement (Caridad Rabelo, Robotham and McCluney 2021). Black women regardless of their life successes and place in life are often disregarded by white men and women who could be decades younger. Black people are taught to respect our elders and treat them with the dignity that they deserve. However, racist white people do not look at our grandparents and elders and see their grandparents with them. You can tell by their actions and the way that they speak that when they see them, they see people who are beneath them regardless of their life experiences and stage of life. If Black women respond to these attacks by whiteness with the same energy that they are receiving, they are instantly labeled as "angry" in an attempt to delegitimize their argument.

Angry, Black, and a Woman, Oh My!

As Dr. Brittney Cooper (2018) puts it, Americans do not recognize that sass is a more digestible form of rage. White people spend so much of their time policing us, but they have never spent any real time respectfully trying to understand us. I am not referring to the white people who study Black people and Black spaces because that is a separate conversation for another day. I am expressly speaking to understanding when we are joking, when we are dead-ass, and when it is just not a good day. Either they cannot read our context clues, or they do not care to. Owning your anger is a dangerous thing (Cooper 2018) for Black people but particularly for Black women. White people have carried this idea with them from the period of enslavement and the idea is that regardless of what they do to us, no matter how harmful it is, that we must keep a cool head. Imagine being theoretically punched in the face every single day and being expected to keep your cool, smile, and be a team player, every single day until you die, or they kill you. It might seem extreme, but I can assure you that having the people responsible for anti-Black racism and white supremacy in command of how you show face in this inevitably cruel world is truly an unavoidable hellscape. We pile so much onto Black women and then wonder they react in ways that are less than gentle. I say, "we" in this context because I am also including Black men in the number of people who labor Black women without thinking twice about how it impacts her well-being. The crisis of loving Black women shows up in all of the critical life spaces that she inhabits where she is often told that she is difficult or underserving of love because of her behavior, complexion, hair texture/length, and size (Gaines 2017). Black women literally and figuratively are never allowed to take a break. Whether it be expectations of her job, society, her relationship, or family; rest is never a luxury afforded to them.

The long-term health concerns of women are absolutely tied to misogynoir and medical racism. If we understand that Black women die at astronomically higher numbers than any other race in childbirth, how have we not figured out how to solve the issue of the medical racism that killed them. From the medical experimentation that took place during the antebellum south to Henrietta Lacks, and the medical malpractice of today this country has never been a safe haven for Black women in any capacity. A great deal of justifiable anger among Black women is because they truly do not feel safe or protected and that is an American problem and a humanitarian issue. The mass media has been complicit in many of the tropes that it has created surrounding Black women (Corbin, Smith and Garcia 2018). As Cooper (2018) mentioned in

Eloquent Rage even the tropes pertaining to Black women on television can become the perception that non-Black women create and an expectation that they carry when they encounter Black women. Black women are not the only marginalized group with the propensity for justified rage, but I do not ever recall hearing any tropes of other women from other colonized groups in the regular media consumption.

Black women are often placed on the defense when they are brought into contact with daily racism in historically and predominately white spaces (Corbin et al. 2018). Popular mass media constantly marks Black women as abusive, controlling, unpredictable, sassy, angry, and strong (Corbin et al. 2018). Which disallows for most people who only engage with Black women through the television and their own assumptions to see their full humanity outside of a caricature. These intentional and pervasive depictions often lack necessary nuance and allow for simplistic interpretations to appear as holistic and truthful depictions of Black women (Corbin et al. 2018). Very similar to the scapegoat hypothesis where a member of the majority group blames their shortcomings on members of marginalized groups. White people have given themselves permission to believe that the lies they told about us are true. If there is any group within the context of the American social experiment poised to understand the sheer brilliance of Africans Americans as a whole, it is white people. White people as a collective despise the assertion that they could remotely be considered racist. What I find most interesting again is that the identification of yourself as "white" is an acceptance of the racialized category which stems from, you guessed it, anti-miscegenation, and white supremacy! Either white people are unaware of their own history, or they just naively claim membership in something because it "seems" cool.

A great deal of European immigrants now categorized as white in the American context had their own battles with white supremacy upon their arrival on this land. The Italians, the Irish, and several other European groups were not immediately welcomed into the category of whiteness when they arrived after the first wave of European immigrants. The Irish were quite literally the last to be included within the category "white," and the only reason that they moved up the racialized hierarchical ladder was because Southern Black folks began moving North during the great migration. Instead of creating space and perhaps a solid allegiance between themselves and African Americans they [the Irish] joined in on the racism when they took on certain professions like policing. Very similar to white women in America the other oppressed groups had no real concern with white supremacists and their tactics of oppression. They would just rather not be the target of the attacks. I have never had the belief system that suffering should be passed onto someone else and believe it or not I do not wish to oppress white people.

Let us be clear, I do not wish to see white people as the majority ruling class, and I wish to see the end of white supremacy and anti-Black racism but that does not mean that I wish to oppress them. You know what that is called? *Answer: Nuance!*

I believe that everyone deserves to have a fair shake at life and white people should not be the deciders of who that should be. I also do not believe that white people have a right to decide who should and should not have access to this country. America always seems to find a way to locate funding to bail our or assist anything that is white-centered. Still, it takes a literal act of Congress for this country to decide to offer any small morsel of assistance or recognition to the only group forced to reside here. African Americans have to wrestle with Americans and non-Americans in their understanding of our very unique lived experience. We are the only group who reside in America by force. And for the record, going back to Africa is not a logistical option for all of the African Americans in this country without further collapsing the infrastructure of Mother Africa. If that was your response or initial thought, you should probably sit this one out. If you had to carry the burden of this knowledge with you every day of your life, would you not also be angry?

When viewing previous course evaluations some of my white students' comments were things like "*he has a chip on his shoulder!*," "*all he talks about is race!*," or "*he's rude!*." What white people fail to realize is that they already have preconceived notions of how we are supposed to be and if we do anything outside of what they deem appropriate they result to name calling or labeling. Particularly if something that they did in the initial interaction prompted your response. There never seems to be any accountability for how we can feel their racism and it is not us overreacting or being sensitive. The same way that a child, or a protective animal can sense when someone has a terrible spirit, we can sense the spirit of a racist even before they speak. We have had centuries of lived experience to teach us how to know when we are encountering white danger. I will never apologize for having that sense today, tomorrow, or ever! White people are so invested in white supremacy that they will try to convince you that their critique of you is rooted in anything but racism. *Miss me with that.*

She Comes in Peace

Black women do not typically enter into spaces looking to cause trouble. It just so happens that when Black women enter into any particular space whiteness jumps out among the people who are present. I have witnessed Black women who teach kindergarten critiqued because of how their clothes fit even when there is no skin showing. Black women basketball coaches are also ridiculed for the way their clothes fit them and the same for Black women who are news anchors. Is it her clothing or is it that you cannot help but to sexualize her mere existence? If seeing a Black woman in a fitted cardigan or her arms exposed makes you hot and bothered or uncomfortable it is a personal issue, and you should keep it to yourself. An aspect of the way Black women are treated is situated within the concept of *dehumanization* which as a result of slavery still allows Black women to be viewed as objects (Anderson, et al. 2018). During the period of enslavement, we know that white enslavers took liberty with enslaved African women and as often as they saw fit. The arrangement of slavery for white men was especially beneficial because he could have any type of African woman *or* man as he saw fit and there was nothing, they could do about it. This perspective did not escape white men simply because the enslaved were free. Instead, it allowed their sexual obsession with the enslaved to be moved from a physical manifestation of their fetish [*ability to rape at will*] toward a mental exercise of the *what-if.* White people are consistently lusting after what they publicly hate but secretly desire.

Thou doth protest too much is what comes to mind when I think about political legislators; what they espouse; and what their Google search histories actually show; particularly in red states. The most hateful legislators come from red states and proclaim themselves to be moving in ways that are faith-based and God-centered. That is what their mouths and political platforms say. Somehow what they pretend to dislike publicly does not coincide with what their constituents value in the privacy of their homes. Red states tend to view more porn than that of blue states (Engelking 2014). There is evidence to suggest that Black people are often dehumanized because we are likened to objects by our oppressors who will always sexualize us (Anderson et al. 2018). The objectification and hypersexualizing of Black women is reminiscent of the treatment of Sarah Bartmann [*Hottentot Venus*], who was an enslaved woman from South Africa (Watson, et al. 2012). Bartmann was trafficked through Europe with her body on display with her buttocks often presented in a way as if she were inviting male attention (Watson et al. 2012). The treatment of Bartmann ultimately led to her untimely death at the age of twenty-six from pneumonia. Even after Bartmann's death in 1815 she was still not allowed to rest in peace. White people kept her brain and her sexual organs on display in a museum in Paris, France until 1974. She was not properly laid to rest until 2002! It is unfathomable to me, that any logical minded white person, would not be able to understand why we feel as strongly as we do about the period of enslavement.

Not being able to be laid to rest for 187 years is just cruel and to think not a single white person thought of it that way is purely enraging. I do not see what was done to Bartmann's remains as any less equivalent to what Dahmer did to the remains of Black men, but the difference is he went to prison for it. No one was ever held accountable, and that rationale is on brand with how and why Black women are treated in such inhumane ways.

The Inhumanity of Black Womanhood and Mothering

The period of enslavement and Black mothering is what charted the path for how white people still consider both Black women and their offspring as disposable. Black women are still considered to be subhuman and how they experience the healthcare system while carrying life is reflective of it. How many stories do we need to hear of Black women who are celebs and some everyday people about their near-death experience while attempting to bring their child earthside before fixing the systemic issue. Black women have a long and storied history of poor maternal outcomes in the United States, and it is directly related to *misogynoir* (Canty 2021). Canty (2021) reminds us that when compared to white women Black women are three times as likely to die from complications pertaining to childbirth.

The question is always why? Why is childbirth for Black women more dangerous than childbirth for any other demographic and in particular white women? It is because when white women say that they are hurting, fearful, or in pain everyone jumps. Whereas when a Black woman says the same thing, she is treated as if she is lying and like she cannot be an advocate for her own body. To understand how widespread systemic racism is it requires of you to use your good common sense and interrogate the obvious inequities. It should not take an act of Congress for Black lives to matter and for Black women to have the respect that they deserve. Additionally, a unique aspect of Black women to white women experiences in childbirth is that even college educated Black women are more likely to have a premature birth than a white woman who has not completed high school (Abrams and Belgrave 2016). African Americans are more likely to be vulnerable to premature health deterioration as a result of coping with consistent stress because of politics, economics, and social exclusion (Abrams and Belgrave 2016). Racism is a literal public health crisis, and it needs to be taken as serious as any other initiative of the last century. With each and every major political and social justice movement that we have we witnessed it appears that the political elites are providing bandages for the wounds without addressing how to stop the wounds from occurring. The concept that we are better than where we were and that the handouts are better than nothing is passive and lazy. I do not need to be pacified and neither should you but what we do need is to see legitimate movement on the liberation front and not incremental growth.

Misogynoir has had a countrywide impact on African American women and their interactions with Western Medicine and the healthcare system (Abrams and Belgrave 2016). With issues like location and transportation barriers, lack of proper and adequate health insurance, poor quality care, and poor communication from healthcare providers (Abrams and Belgrave 2016). Each of these inequities are the difference between life and death for African American women and require much more attention than they have been given. Despite public advocacy aimed at increasing health care access for marginalized groups the research is still limited on how this approach can be mimicked for African American women (Abrams and Belgrave 2016). I am irrevocably saddened by this because it is all intentional and absolutely preventable. Black women deserve so much more from this country! So much more. A heartbreaking aspect of all of this is the fact that as a result of white supremacy and anti-Black racism, Black people would rather avoid health screenings than to be subjected to violence.

The centuries of medical atrocities inflicted upon African Americans by white people has made the distrust of the healthcare system and modern medicine rampant (Abrams and Belgrave 2016). We all know an Auntie, Uncle, Grandmother, or Grandfather who refused to see a doctor, because they simply do not trust them. White people blame African Americans for their own health disparities without ever considering the cause of the distrust being their anti-Blackness. The stories of exploitation from the antebellum era for African American women, bodies being stolen from graves for dissection, and being deceived into taking part in dangerous experimentations all play a role in the distrust (Abrams and Belgrave 2016). The United States has spent a great bit of time forcing African American women into subjugation simply because they could. It is now time for the United States and the people who inhabit it to place some *R-E-S-P-E-C-T* on the names of the constant saviors of democracy. *Black women!*

REFERENCES

Abrams, Jasmine A., and Faye C. Belgrave. 2016. "Reducing Disparities and Achieving Equity in African American Women's Health." *American Psychologist, Vol. 71 No.8* 723–733.

Anderson, Joel R., Elise Holland, Courtney Heldreth, and Scott P. Johnson. 2018. "Revisiting the Jezebel Stereotype: The Impact of Target Race on Sexual Objectification." *Psychology of Women Quarterly, Vol. 42. Issue 4* 461–476.

Canty, Lucinda. 2021. "The lived experience of severe maternal morbidity among Black women." *Nursing Inquiry* 1–15.

Caridad Rabelo, Verónica, Kathrina J. Robotham, and Courtney L. McCluney. 2021. "Gender, Bodies and Identities in Organizations: Postcolonial Critiques: 'Against a sharp white background': How Black women experience the white gaze at work." *Gender Work Organ, 28* 1840–1858.

Cooper, Brittney. 2018. "The Problem with Sass." In *Eloquent Rage: A Black Feminist Discovers Her Superpower*, by Brittney Cooper, 1–7. New York: St. Martins Press.

Corbin, Nicole A., William A. Smith, and Roberto Garcia. 2018. "Trapped between justified anger and being the strong Black woman: Black college women coping with racial battle fatigue at historically and predominantly White institutions." *International Journal of Qualitative Studies in Education,31:7* 626–643.

Engelking, Carl. 2014. *People in Religious and Conservative States Seek Out More Pornography Online.* December 30. https://www.discovermagazine.com/mind/people-in-religious-and-conservative-states-seek-out-more-pornography-online.

Gaines, Zeffie. 2017. "A Black Girl's Song Misogynoir, Love, and Beyoncé's Lemonade." *Taboo: The Journal of Culture and Education* 97–114.

Johnson, Ahjah Marie. 2022. "Grown Black Woman Voice: A Framework for Existence, Persistence, Resistance in Higher Education and Beyond." *Journal of African American Women and Girls in Education, Vol. 2 No.2* 86–100.

Stouffer-Lerch, Sarah. 2020. *The Hidden History of Ohio State's Black Student Body.* https://odi.osu.edu/hidden-history-ohio-states-black-student-body#:~:text=By%20the%201950s%2C%20the%20university,done%20to%20desegregate%20campus%20housing.

Watson, Laurel, Dawn Robinson, Franco Dispenza, and Negar Nazari. 2012. "African American Women's Sexual Objectification Experiences: A Qualitative Study." *Psychology of Women Quarterly. Vol 36 Issue 4* 468–475.

West, Emily, and R.J. Knight. 2017. "Mothers' Milk: Slavery, Wet-Nursing, and Black and White Women in the Antebellum South." *The Journal of Southern History,83,1* 37–68.

Williams, Apryl. 2020. "Black Memes Matter: #LivingWhileBlack With Becky and Karen." *Social Media + Society, Vol. 6 Issue 4.*

Chapter 6

Strange Fruit

History of Black Feminism

AIN'T I A WOMAN?

Misogynoir although a modern term has existed in different variations since the enslaved first arrived in this country. Isabella Baumfree a.k.a. "Sojourner Truth" declared "*Ain't I a Woman?*" during her 1851 speech at the Women's Convention in Akron, Ohio. Truth's speech was her way of highlighting the importance of Black women's shared cause in feminism. Traditional white feminism has always been problematic because it failed to recognize the concerns and the voices of Black and other marginalized women. A perspective that is largely missing from traditional feminism which is centered in whiteness is that other women have issues that exist beyond patriarchy. It is expressly why *intersectionality,* which was coined by legal scholar Kimberlé Crenshaw, is important because it recognizes the nuanced experiences of Black womanhood. Very similar to the erasure and redefining of *misogynoir* by other people *intersectionality* has experienced the same revisionist history and white washing.

Intersectionality was founded in the 1980s by Crenshaw and intended to focus its efforts on the vexed dynamics of differences and the solidarities of sameness (Cho, Crenshaw, and McCall 2013). Each entity being necessary to understand social-movement politics and anti-discrimination contexts (Cho et al. 2013). According to Cho et al., (2013), it exposed how single-axis thinking [*like feminism vs. patriarchy*] undermines legal thinking and does not provide any space for nuance or counternarratives of the *othered.* A key perspective to always tuck away in your memory cap, I have expressed it in this book, and I will do it here, white women never cared about the oppression of other women. White women wanted to make sure that it would be clear that they should be equal to white men. This perspective alone is enough to turn traditional white feminism on its head. Failure to include race, racism, and white supremacy in any discourse that seems to disrupt status-quo is anti-Black and self-serving. Throughout the last three decades, intersectionality has proved to be a productive concept deployed in various academic disciplines like history, sociology, feminist studies, higher education, ethnic studies, queer studies, and anthropology to name a few (Cho et al. 2013). Intersectionality insists upon the examination of sameness and the dynamics of difference and how each has facilitated creating dialogue around race, gender, and other axes of power in politics, academics, and new developments in more non-traditional fields like geography (Cho et al. 2013).

Intersectionality as an intellectual and socio-societal pushback against traditional feminism raises questions [for some] regarding a number of issues: limitations and utility of its various metaphors including the matrix, road intersection, the interlocked vision of oppression; and the autonomous versus interactive and mutually constituting nature of the gender; class; race; sexuality; nation nexus; the & thing or the etc. [*et cetera*] problem (Cho et al. 2013). As Cho et al., (2013) further states, some of the more present critiques of intersectionality revolve around its ability to do anything other than call attention to the particularities and erasure of Black women. *The audacity!* The only people that truly critique feminism across the larger society are white men and women who hate the idea of aligning with other women while upholding patriarchy. Who critiques intersectionality? Everybody! Why? Because how dare there exist a theoretical and practical approach that allows for us to understand how Black women are intentionally forced into the margins of society, silenced, consistently oppressed, and even murdered for daring to exist in any way but as a servant to men.

As usual anything aimed at uplifting, highlighting, and drawing space for the existence of Blackness has to be critiqued by the whole of society whether or not the critics are worthy of acknowledgment or have ulterior motives aimed at being purely contrarian. Since the inception of intersectionality, it has been posed more as a nodal point rather than a closed system [*like white feminism*], a gathering place for open-ended investigations of the overlapping and conflicting dynamics of nation, gender, race, sexuality, and class (Cho et al. 2013). The aforementioned dimensions allows for there to exist multi-dynamic discourse surrounding the very essential needs of Black women and women of color free of the white gaze and approval.

CRENSHAW MADE IT PLAIN

Americans and by the absence of race specificity I mean, white people. Have always made decisions and created scholarship regarding African Americans in ways that were both paternalistic and deficit framed. In the creation of *intersectionality* Kimberlé Crenshaw made her intentions clear and plain. Crenshaw (1989) states, her intention was to center Black women in this analysis [*legal discourse regarding anti-discrimination*] in order to be able to contrast the multidimensionality of Black women's experiences. This juxtaposition was intended to reveal how Black women were theoretically erased, and how this framework imports its own theoretical limitations that undermine efforts to broaden anti-racist and feminist analysis (Crenshaw 1989). In her argument Crenshaw (1989) insisted that focusing on the most privileged group members, marginalized those who are burdened by multiple marginalized identities and obscures claims that cannot be understood as a result of discrete sources of discrimination free of racism. Prior to Crenshaw's disruption the conversation that centered around anti-racism and sexism were often singularly focused and did not allow for the inclusion of the additional others.

Crenshaw (1989) further states that simply lumping in Black women within an already established analytical structure would only further exclude them. Imagine being invited to an already planned international trip within a group of acquaintances who you speak to from time to time. Consider that they have already planned all of the excursions for the trip (dinner, lodging, social events, and travel) and then you are asked to attend, if you want to. It does not give you the warm and fuzzy's and it makes you feel like you were last considered or perhaps a replacement for a person who they actually preferred to invite. That was how white feminism as a framework looked when attempting to include Black women without fully considering and acknowledging their needs. Understanding intersectionality means understanding that it as Crenshaw puts it, is greater than the sum of sexism and racism. She furthered argued that for anti-racist policy discourse and feminist theory to fully embrace the concerns and lived experiences of Black women that the approach would need to be recast and reconsidered (Crenshaw 1989). One salient departure from any connection to feminism for Black women has been the preference to be labeled a *womanist* instead.

FEMINIST OR WOMANIST APPROACHES FOR BLACK WOMEN

Black women stood at a crossroads in regard to how to define their ever present need to be both seen and heard (Collins 1996). Powerhouse Black women put words and psalm to paper to allow us to be able to conceptualize, interrogate, theorize, and put into practice necessary ways to understand the vitality and softness of Black womanhood. Black women used the period of the '70s and '80s as an opportunity to *talk back* and to allow themselves to be seen and for the first time to not choose silence. As a condition of American Black womanhood there always existed a keen belief that similar to children, Black women were to be seen and not heard. This less than humanly value also rested with white women but with them rested one perceivably exceptional condition and that was *whiteness*. For Black women there was no escaping the swift hand of both patriarchy and racism regardless of where they resided. The only taste of safety that would be provided for Black women would be if their landing place did not include men. Men provided a particular risk for Black women that disallows for there to ever exist a time for Black women to be vocal about her political, social, and personal beliefs that were not either the beliefs of her father or her partner. Before you get your boxers in a bunch my brothas you must pause and ask yourself if you, yourself, have ever or could ever be a place of safety for Black women. Many of you believe this about yourself and it is largely because you are not self-aware. A great deal of our sistas if you listen closely enough to them have almost never felt safe in this country. If that is not something that hits you right in the gut, there is not much you could offer this discussion. Black women who did not have a safe place to land more times than not do not know how to create a safe place to land for you. That is of no fault of her own and it is not meant as a tactic to throw at her in a fight. I say that as a reminder for you to taper your own feelings in this moment and to just listen more and speak less.

When Black women began to finally speak out their voices became provocative and as Collins (1996) mentions, their words were welcomed in higher education classrooms, but they were not. Very similar to faux DEI initiatives of today the '70s and '80s were also performative in that institutions of higher learning believed in the symbolism of change but not the praxis of it (Collins 1996). Every day institutional polices and approaches continued to be exclusionary to Black women as more and more academic institutions adopted and pushed their work (Collins 1996). As Black women began to make sense of all that they have in common along with what separated them in arenas like class, sexuality, religion, region, and nationality, there existed a reality that their solidarity was essential (Collins 1996). During that time period debates were had as to what to refer to the collective standpoint of Black women as and if it should be called *Black feminism or womanism* as the most appropriate collective term (Collins 1996). Alice Walker's work in *In Search of our Mothers' Gardens* (1983) introduced four meanings of the *womanist* (Collins 1996). In her [Walker's] first definition she stated that a womanist was a Black feminist *or* a feminist of color which provided an understanding of the interchangeability of the word (Collins 1996). Very similar to Walker, there are some Black women who see no difference between the two because each highlight and supports a common agenda of Black women's self-determination and self-agenda (Collins 1996). During that period there was discussion about separating the two and defining them individually particularly for Black women who placed themselves in separate camps of each (Collins 1996).

WOMANISM

Walker viewed womanism as rooted in Black women's concrete history in both gender and racialized oppression (Collins 1996). She considered the term "womanish" as something that Southern Black mothers would say to their daughters whom they believed to be acting in a womanly way free of restriction (Collins 1996). As a New Yorker, I do not recall hearing Black women in my family using the term "womanish," but I have most assuredly heard them tell a young Black girl to stop acting "grown." The term "grown" was often used to indicate that the child was acting in ways that could and or would bring her the wrong kind of attention from older men. I am often troubled by this term primarily because it places the onus of responsibility on young ladies instead of the grown ass men who pursued them. In fact, Black girls and women were always blamed for the ways that older age-inappropriate men found them attractive. Thinking back to my own adolescence I remember when we were in middle-school and young ladies in my class who were about twelve or thirteen years of age who had boyfriends who were anywhere between 17–22 years of age. I thought it was really weird that nearly grown men and actually adult men had any remote interest in girls within our peer group but had no idea it was illegal. Quite a few of those young ladies shared and fought over the same boyfriend and many became mothers before they turned 16. The women in the community just called them "fast" but no one ever said anything to or about the men who impregnated them.

Womanist were considered to be the take charge type of Black women who could be considered courageous or outrageous in deliberate ways which broke them free from the confines that trapped white women (Collins 1996). Womanish girls in Walker's terms wanted to know more and knowing more was considered a bad thing for Black women which made them responsible, in charge, and serious (Collins 1996). Walker intentionally constructed Black women's experiences in contradiction of and in opposition to white women which by default made womanism *superior* to feminism (Collins 1996). The difference was said to stem from both Black and white women's histories with racism in the American context and further syphoning off how we define womanhood and race (Collins 1996). Walker used the explanation of *womanist is to feminist as purple is to lavender* which seemed poised to say that Black women are "womanist" and white women are simply "feminist" (Collins 1996). According to Collins (1996) this very pointed perspective sits very squarely in the realm of Black nationalist traditions that posit that Black people and white people cannot function as equals. This is primarily due to the fact that white people's sole purpose in any relationship with Black folks is to create a sense of subjugation which they are vested in as a result of white supremacy (Collins 1996). Womanism allows for Black women to remain distanced from those who seek to do them harm [the enemy] (Collins 1996). Womanism intended to sidestep the issue of interracial cooperation because its sole focus was on Black women and the embracing of nationalist philosophies and had little interest in working with white women (Collins 1996). It is important to note that as an ethical system, womanism is always in the making and it is not a closed fixed system of ideas but one that continually evolves through its rejection of all forms oppression with a deep commitment to social justice (Collins 1996). I would like to take this time to address something that I am sure might be a point of contention for some of you as you journey through this book. I am a truth teller and part of that disruptive obligation means to directly name the things that for reasons of performance or respectability others refuse to name. There can be no reconciliation of racism if the only option is that we, the descendants of the enslaved, simply just drop the subject. For many people, their core belief system is the avoidance of difficult topics of discussion. Our existence in this country is relegated to being forever subjugated by whiteness and those who have membership within it. Like many of the Black women who chose not to be silent and refused to be quiet in the face of oppression, as do I. I seek no approval in whiteness, white systems, or white people. I seek only to engage productively with my white peers and co-conspirators who have decided to journey along with us on our journey toward liberation.

As I often tell my students regarding racism and white supremacy, no part of this discussion is easy. Many of you will become extremely uncomfortable and you might squirm in your seat or put the book down completely. All of those feelings are fine as long as you are able to sit with the reality, unsexy, non-cookie cutter version of the truth. Most white people who engage the conversation of white supremacy and racism feel like they are doing us a favor by allowing us space to talk about it, and that is where they are all wrong. You are doing yourself the favor by being open to hearing about and learning about the truth. The truth might not set you free, but it will most certainly set you straight. This conversation will forever be uneasy, but it will always be necessary, avoidance is not the move. An additional aspect of Black women's multiuse of the term womanism is the concern for the slippage between reality and the *what if* (Collins 1996). Being able to identify liberatory *potential* within the communities of Black women that emerges from concrete experiences that are historical is different than pretending that Black women have *arrived* at their most "ideal" *womanist* endpoint (Collins 1996).

BLACK FEMINISM

Varying interpretations of the term *Black feminism* also exists for African American women (Collins 1996). Pearl Cleage defines feminism as, the belief that women are full human beings who are capable of both leadership and participation in the full range of all human endeavor be they social, sexual, political, economic, or intellectual (Collins 1996). In its most broad sense, feminism is comprised of both a global political movement and an ideology that confronts sexism, which in this context is a social relationship where the male group has authority over the female group (Collins 1996). In a global worldview a feminist agenda covers the following areas: economic status of women; women's global poverty; political rights; and basic human rights violations like rape and torture is the second area of concern (Collins 1996). The third area of concern globally hinges upon family and marital issues such as marriage and divorce laws, child custody policies, and also domestic labor (Collins 1996). Women's health and survival issues (*reproductive rights, pregnancy, AIDS, and sexuality*) constitute another area of the global feminist agenda although varying expressions can exist among the world and diverse populations (Collins 1996).

By using the term *Black feminism,* it positions African American women to examine how the issues that directly impact women factor into women's emancipation struggles globally (Collins 1996). An issue that exists within the context of feminism and the global stage is that the media in the United States constantly portrays feminism as a *whites only* movement and white women never offered to disrupt it (Collins 1996). White women did not debate the attention that this worldwide caption gave them because for once they had something that they were not required to share with men. White feminism relies on being centered, seen, and heard without any regard for the struggle of others and that perspective alone is on brand with white supremacy. Despite the media erasure, African American women have long struggled to be seen in the fight to raise the standing and notability of what appeared to be whites-only-feminism (Collins 1996). The African American women who have long participated in feminist work have always contended with their erasure in the media and from their white counterparts all while leading and helping to found feminist orgs like NOW [*Pauli Murray*] (Collins 1996).

One of the things that Pearl Cleage espoused, and I wholeheartedly agree with is that being a *feminist* simply means that you believe in the social, political, and legal equality of women (Collins 1996). As cisgender men we often hear patriarchal fools refer to us as Beta males because we believe that women have just as much say so in this world as men. Moreover, the belief that women are just as intelligent as men if not the most intelligent of the two. For many men who refuse to do the reading they believe that being a feminist or even a womanist means that you hate men. To be a Black feminist places your thought process more in alignment with equity, justice, fairness, anti-oppression, and abolition which by definition means that it is not possible to hate men. In fact, when I think about Black feminism and more importantly *intersectional feminism,* I think about the act of love and that love being situated squarely in all that you do with and for your people in this fight for liberation. Love for your people does not allow you to hate them. It requires of you to hold them in high regard and to hold them accountable. For many men, accountability equals hatred and that is about as foolish as equating accountability to cancel culture. Both arguments stem from one party attempting to protect their right to treat you [the marginalized] any type of way without you having any recourse. *Grow up!*

Using the term *Black feminism* is intentional because its aim is to disrupt the racism which is inherent in the presentation of feminism as a for whites only ideology and political movement (Collins 1996). The insertion of "Black" in the term is also poised to highlight the contradictions underlying in the assumption of whiteness in feminism and to remind white women that they do not have a monopoly on feminists (Collins 1996). bell hooks taught us as Black men that we could break the life-threatening choke hold that patriarchal masculinity places upon Black men and create life sustaining visions of a reconstructed masculinity that provides a way for Black men to save our lives and the lives of our brothers and sisters (Lemons 1997). I think about this often and more specifically about how I navigate my relationships with both women and men. I am often complimented by Black women because of how I take up for Black women and in my deepest place I do not believe that I need the praise. I do not feel that I need or am deserving of praise because I do what I feel that we all should when it pertains to being in relationship with and to each other. My relationships with the women in my life are gifts. And even with the very complicated relationship that I share with my own mother because of her past hurts it does not cause me to aim or seek to harm all the Black women in my wake.

Black women have always been my sounding board as far back as I can remember. My earliest relationship with a woman other than my mother is the one that I have with my sister who is very special to me. My mom says that she and I were inseparable almost instantly and us being close in age also plays a part in it. I believe that women are angels that God allows us to borrow and to form hedges of protection around us in this hellscape on earth. I value Black women deep. I value the Black women and their strength that allowed them to endure in spite of it all. Sometimes I sit and think about the prayers of my grandmothers, and I wish I could hear the things that they dreamt for their future generations. I believe in some distant part of me that they were praying for me even before they knew me or before I existed. That is how honored I feel to be able to honor Black women. When I hear the way that some Black men talk about Black women all I feel is a deep sadness because behind all of that vitriol is a hurt little boy. A little boy desperately needed to be loved deeply by his mother and perhaps because of the weight of the world and how much the world hated her, he believed that she hated him too. I feel a perpetual sadness that the work of white supremacy in our lives has been so violent and so constant that so many of us are incapable of recognizing it.

Just as Black women and Black men are hypersexualized, I believe that Black men are also hyper-masculinized which creates a constant fear that someone in some mysterious way is attempting to emasculate him. I feel sorry for men whose heterosexism is so fragile that the idea that a woman rejecting him means that she no longer deserves to live. I feel sorry that heterosexism and homophobia are so rampant that the idea of being gentle and loving with your children who might be queer [*or perhaps not*] causes people to question the sexuality of a caring dad. I am thankful for the father that I have because he, although far from perfect, never taught me to be toxic, to degrade women, or to belittle other men who might be far less masculine than me. I pray for the awakening in my brothas who feel that being hard all the time is necessary or essential to establish their dominance. I can assure you that no one feels safe when you act like a caveman even if they lie to you and tell you that they do. You are capable and deserving of love and I hope that you believe that too.

THE COMBAHEE RIVER COLLECTIVE

The Combahee River Collective were a group of Black feminists who began meeting together in 1974. The purpose of their meeting was for them to clarify and more accurately define their politics while simultaneously doing political activist work within their own group and in coalition with other progressive movements and organizations (Smith 1979). The women of the group made it clear that their politics were situated in struggling against sexual, racial, heterosexual, and class oppression and believed it for not to be their shared responsibility to development and integrated analysis and practice on the interlocking systems of oppression (Smith 1979). As stated by Smith (1979) the synthesis of the aforementioned oppressions created the conditions of their lived experiences. The collective defined that their origins consisted of being situated in Afro-American women's continuous life-and-death struggle for survival and also liberation (Smith 1979). What stands out for me in this collective statement is a shared vision and that is that white male rule in this world is both physically, emotionally, spiritually, and economically damaging to us all. Our collective and continued oppression is because one singular group decided that it is and shall always be so.

Black feminist politics also situate themselves in obvious ways to the struggle and movements for Black liberation most particularly the movements of the '60s and '70s (Smith 1979). It was their participation in those movements that helped the collective to realize that they needed to be both anti-racist [*due to white women*] and anti-sexist [*due to Black and white men*] (Smith 1979). The collective also knew that their development was necessary and for that reason needed to be tied to Black liberatory movements. All of our liberation is conditional if we all do not realize the greater purpose of it all. We cannot move individually, and it makes this discovery shine a brighter light on why we cannot disqualify our people from fighting alongside us simply because they look, live, and love differently than we do.

STRANGE FRUIT

Billie Holiday sung about *strange fruit* as a way to highlight the ills of the Black lived experience via lynching while also critiquing how white supremacy snuffs out Black people without consequence. As a result of Holiday's resistance toward white supremacy she faced countless acts of misogynoir throughout her career. *Strange Fruit* as a term today can be used to highlight how Black womanhood is commercialized for profit all while snuffing out the voices of Black women and their struggle for liberation. The Combahee Collective, Alice Walker, Patricia Hill Collins, bell hooks, Moya Bailey, Billie Holiday, and countless other Black women spend their entire lives teaching us all how to recognize and even to avoid the *strange fruit*. Billie was so unmovable in her core belief to tell the truth about lynching and the anti-Black racism that inhabited this country. We all exist in a country that constantly shows us at every turn how easy it is for them to snap their fingers and end our lives.

When we consider the antics and the efforts of the southern states and midwestern red states we have to consider the double entendre of *strange fruit* as code for forbidden knowledge. White people dislike when Black people are self-aware and what they dislike more than a Black person who is self-aware is a Black person with a platform and ability to awaken others. Holiday's strange fruit which was recorded in 1939 was originally written by Abel Meeropol who was an English teacher in Brooklyn, New York (Carvalho 2013). Meeropol wrote the poem under his pen name Lewis Allan and published it in *The New York Teacher* in January of 1937 (Carvalho 2013). Holiday had an intimate relationship to the song because of her own experiences as a Black woman in America. Early in her life Holiday experienced the ills of being Black and a girl when she was raped and then institutionalized as punishment for her own sexual assault (Carvalho 2013). Holiday like the women in the Collective and other Black queer feminists were brought to a point of contention with the dichotomy that exists between their physical bodies [*made sexual*] and the politics of their Blackness. Black women have always been placed in proximity to harm when it comes to their bodies and their ability to determine with whom and if they want to have sex. I do not think most men utterly understand that Black women reside in a constant state of fear because men do not aim to control themselves when they have determined that something belongs to them. Patriarchy and white supremacy are the cause of it all!

As Black people we all carry the potential to be harmed simply for existing, but no one carries this burden within our community more than Black women and queer people. Billie's staying power in the resistance made her a target by the federal government just like it did with Dr. King, Malcolm X, The Black Panthers, and countless others. Billie's drug and alcohol misuse was because she used them to cope with both white supremacy and the trauma of her rape. Henry Anslinger was the Commissioner of the Federal Bureau of Narcotics for more than thirty years. Anslinger was also a notorious racist, used his power, like most white men in government to target and harass Holiday. He used the n-word so religiously that elected officials of the day believed that he was not fit to be in office, but no one stopped him or his harassment of Holiday. *Sound familiar?* Per usual, white men will behave badly while other white people disagree with them and do nothing about it. One of the integral aspects for white people who consider themselves to be co-conspirators in the fight for liberation is knowing that simply disagreeing with white supremacy is not sufficient enough. What actionable steps are you willing to take to either assist the marginalized or eliminate the possibility of any harm before it becomes an issue? A co-conspirator must not only be reactionary they must also be proactive, and that work is constant. The work of resistance must be as steadfast as the work of anti-Black racism and white supremacy. The hatred of our humanity has never allowed us to not resist. If you consider yourself to be anti-racist and a co-conspirator, how have you assisted Black women? In what ways have you used your racialized privilege to actively assist someone of color and legitimately not expect anything in return, even their loyalty. *I have asked this before and I will ask it again, what are you willing to give up?*

REFERENCES

Carvalho, John M. 2013. "'Strange Fruit': Music between Violence and Death." *The Journal of Aesthetics and Art Criticism* 111–119.

Cho, Sumi, Kimberlé' Crenshaw, and Leslie McCall. 2013. "Toward a Field of Intersectional Studies: Theory, Applications, and Praxis." *Signs, 38* 785–810.

Collins, Patricia Hill. 1996. "WHAT'S IN A NAME? Womanism, Black Feminism, and Beyond." *The Black Scholar Journal of Black Studies and Research, 26:* 19–17.

Crenshaw, Kimberlé. 1989. "Demarginalizing the Intersection of Race and Sex: A Black Feminist Critique of Antidiscrimination Doctrine, Feminist Theory and Antiracist Politics." *The University of Chicago Legal Forum* 139–167.

Lemons, Gary. 1997. "To be Black, Male, and 'Feminist'—Making Womanist Space for Black Men." *International Journal of Sociology and Social Policy,Volume 17 Number 1/2* 35–61.

Smith, Barbara. 1979. "Combahee River Collective: A Black Feminist Statement." *Off Our Backs Vol. 9. No.6* 6–8.

Chapter 7

Glory

How to Join the Resistance

IT WILL BE OURS

John Legend and Common's award-winning song *Glory* from the film *Selma* served to highlight the movement toward Black liberation and how justice is more than a one-time occurrence. Our fight for liberation must be ongoing until we all see freedom. If you have been reading this book in full process, then you are beginning or already know why standing down is not an option. The war over our liberation is not nearly concluded and it requires for us to be faithful and steadfast until we see victory. The elder's wisdom is essential to understanding where we have come from, but the energy and vigor of the youth is what will be needed to physically keep up our fight. We each have a role in our resistance and fight for liberation and us all at times need some specificity on how to become clear about what our role is.

A reoccurring dialogue within the Black community is that certain elements of resistance do not work (voting, protesting, civil unrest). However, these statements are often made by the oppressors or by marginalized members who buy into the concept of respectability. If voting did not work and if civil unrest does not work, then explain why white people lose their complete shyt when we participate in either of them? What must be understood is that freedom is not always a peaceful agreement and you certainly do not ask for your oppressor's permission about how to proceed toward liberation. Freedom for any nation of oppressed people rarely occurred based on an ask and an acknowledgment. Freedom often arrived due to uprising and bloodshed. Although I am certainly *not* calling for war, I am simply reminding you that historically anything in this country that required disruption did not happen until the disruption [*in various forms*] took place. Understanding that each marginalized person and group has a role in the battle for liberation is essential. Standing on the sidelines and criticizing without understanding is not one of those necessary roles. Encouraging African Americans to be more politically aware will allow each of us to be better stewards of our vote. It will also encourage us to vote in a way that benefits the least of us which will certainly provide protections for all of us. There is no liberation when the most privileged among us feels no sense of responsibility and connection for the most disadvantaged of us. We are each other's responsibility, and we need to join in the fight to save us all. This I earnestly believe, and I absolutely will look at you with concern if you do not grasp this most basic concept. There is no possible way that reconciliation or a true peaceful existence can occur between the oppressed and the oppressors without accountability and an intentional and meaningful resolution occurs.

Requiring the oppressed to forget about our past as we watch the purveyors and beneficiaries of white supremacy belittle and diminish democracy at every turn is disrespectful. You have the Governors of many of these states signing anti-CRT laws knowing full well that CRT is *not* in any way taught in K-12 education. Hell, unless you have a fire ass professor you still will not deeply engage with it in undergrad. Most scholars of critical race who also teach it do not engage the material with anyone but graduate and professional students. What they are actually banning is student's ability to learn about the more basic concepts of American and Black history which is truly American history. White legislators want to teach fantasy stories about the United States as a safe haven and a place built on progressive thinking all while silencing the most progressive in the political arena. Quite literally none of this makes sense, none of it! The privilege of whiteness allows both political parties to applaud themselves for either disrupting progress or only making incremental changes and then looking at us for approval like Stuart on *MADtv*. It is unconscionable to constantly ask the descendants of the enslaved to support you and keep you elected and then force us to watch you never address issues that directly impact us. To this end, I have seen several famous rappers try and encourage us to hold our votes until we [*Black people*] receive what we are owed and what we have been asking for. The only issue I have with that is that they only raise these concerns *during* an election year. Part of being proactive is having these conversations earlier on and organizing to make certain that issues pertaining to our liberation are addressed within the first ninety days. Withholding your vote and or sitting out on election days because you believe your vote does not matter is something that I wholeheartedly disagree with. There are absolutely ways that we can apply pressure on our electorate, but it cannot be only during an election year or if it solely benefits you. That is not liberatory that is selfishness.

Being in critique of all politicians and more particularly the liberal agenda allows me as a progressive person to acknowledge their shortcomings. It is completely out of touch for a young Black person to be killed and instead of acknowledging it the President tells us about how low unemployment numbers are, that inflation is being addressed, and that gas prices are declining. All of these things are important, but these things are primarily the concerns of white people and out of touch and selfish non-white persons. It is absolutely true about being *conscious* and in a *rage* a great majority of the time. Primarily because we live in a country that continuously oppresses us and then tells us it could be worse. Liberalism would be more ideal if it was not so performative. I believe liberal politicians and primarily the ones who refer to themselves as "moderate" spend more of their time catering to white people on the margins of democrat and republican as if they are the people who are largely voting them into office. The republicans are clear about who their base is and what sorts of things will rile up their base and get them active. Meanwhile, the democrats who are considered to be the party of the marginalized always fail in their ability to fight in the ways that we would actually like them to. There exists a constant fear of losing the white vote and appeasing them. Democrats fail to realize that if African American men and women stop showing up to the polls altogether, they would never win another election. Knowing this information, they should be fighting like hell that any state that seeks to dilute or dismantle our rights has a fight on their hands at every legislative level.

THEY ARE STILL KILLING US!

When I think of co-conspirators in the fight for liberation, I think of a person who with every fiber of their existence and privilege they are raising the awareness of anti-Black racism and highlight everywhere and every way that it shows up. White supremacy does not just kill us in the streets with a firearm held by the police. White supremacy also kills us in the classroom, in the workplace, at the doctor's office, and in the supermarket. Core to my belief of what it takes to be a co-conspirator is my belief that most people have no earthly idea how dangerous white supremacy is or how it shows up. The knowledge of that alone is enough to send me into a fit. You do not have to call someone the n-word to be racist and an upholder of white supremacy. You also do not need to be in a hooded sheet under the cloak of night to uphold it either. White supremacy is upheld every day in ways that people do not pay attention to. Many African American children's first experience with white supremacy is through their teachers' personal biases and the carceral like operations of their school. In states like Texas where the GOP is fighting ridiculously hard to make all aspects of education white centered and everything else not optional. In the same states that do not want children learning about different aspects of Black history and America's racist past [and present] they also employ white teachers who tell middle schoolers that their own race [white] is superior. I recall a time earlier on in my career where I desperately wanted to teach high school social studies. I lived in Charlotte, N.C. during my undergraduate years and for some time afterward and during that time you needed to have at least eighteen credits of a social science in order to be eligible to teach [social studies] in CMS. I had the credentials but there was no availability in that subject area most of the time. I let that dream go and went on to do other things. I am reminded of how difficult it is for African Americans to enter the classroom in most places and then I watch videos like the one at Bohls Middle School in Pflugerville and I am gob smacked. America makes it entirely too easy for white people to perpetuate harm against Black students and students of color while making it difficult and nearly impossible to employ teachers who look like them. None of this is by accident and it is certainly all done by design. For the co-conspirators who are reading this and work in education I wonder how do you go about eliminating barriers to hire teachers of color and most importantly culturally aware teachers? Is it your assumption that all teachers are inherently good with a mixture of some bad apples or are you more realistic and understand that racists do not check their biases at the door?

When considering the full scope of the American educational system and its intersecting relationship with the school-to-prison pipeline it is hard to fathom that the exclusion of teachers of color and culturally aware teachers is not intentional. Very similar to some Black folks who become police officers there are also anti-Black-Black educators who feel that it is their role to infuse politics of respectability into Black students. As I often say you do not have to be white to uphold white supremacy and that is why this text is important. The experiences of African American children of today and recent years is a deep departure from that of our elders [*pre-Brown v. Board*] in that their educators were African American women which means that the learning of the students was culturally responsive (Watson and Baxley 2021). From the earliest work of Black scholars like Carter G. Woodson we have always known that there existed a duality of biases and unjustness in the American education system (Watson and Baxley 2021). Black children are often subjected to "learning" from people who actually hate them.

As a Black child you could always sense when a white teacher was in your corner and when one of them had it out for you. Throughout my own education I can think of about three different white women teachers who I absolutely felt did not like me and they were my 2nd grade teacher, 4th grade teacher, and 7th grade English teacher. Their patience with me always seemed short and there was definitely no feeling of safety when I was with them. I recall my older brother having several teachers who always tried making him a problem student. My brother nor I were problem students and as I am now old enough to recognize their responses to us were rooted in anti-Blackness. I remember being in middle school and our school having a bit of a zero-tolerance policy regarding being late to school or talking in class.

I recall having to serve ISS (in school suspension) if the option for staying after school was not an option for me. When you were given afterschool detention one of the teachers would go around and round up the students and walk us in a single-file-line through the school picking up the other students. The images and practices of prison culture even for people who themselves had never been, were very present for us. The more well-off presenting white students were almost never in detention of any form. The only white kids who were in detention were the ones who were certifiably outliers. The white girl who was fifteen years old when the average age of 8th graders was thirteen was frequently present as well as the white boys who were frequently caught smoking on school grounds. They were essentially the castaways in comparison to the rest of the white students at the school. The differences between them and their peers was obvious. As I think back throughout all of my K-12 educational experiences I can barely thinking of a time when I had the privilege of a Black administrator outside of when I attended [*wait for it* . . .] Dr. Martin Luther King Jr. elementary school. I think the running joke remains that for some odd reason all roads, streets, and schools named after Dr. MLK Jr. are most assuredly in the hood and I am sure that it is not by accident. I think the government must have decided to draw the redlines directly around anything named after the good brother.

Working in education is hard and as an educator myself, I can certainly understand the difficulties of many days. However, regardless of how difficult of a day I might be having or what the world is doing to me I have to take that energy and spin it into something educational. When I speak about my own lived experiences with anti-Blackness and white supremacy it allows me to paint visual interpretations that many of my students who are not Black or of color have ever experienced. I use my lived experiences to make their educational relatability to anti-Blackness palpable. I am reminded that for most of my students I am the first time that they have seen themselves in an educator. For others, it is the first time that they have seen a Black educator of any kind and that is not lost on me. When I am engaging in discussion with my students I ask as many questions as I can to draw out of them their experiences which helps me to understand where exactly they are on their journey. At times, I am floored by the knowledge and even heartbreaking lived experiences that show up in conversation when they are allowed space free of judgement. It is also in those spaces where I am able to create an education on the importance of language and why we do not use deficit framed and oppressive words. Words like inmate, felon, and ex-con that paint pictures of people as less than when incarcerated person and formerly incarcerated person are free to use.

Believe it or not I have to still wrestle with people using the word "colored" as a means of describing people of color and namely African Americans. I have had to redirect students in their language at more than one university that I have taught at. It is a wonder that folks let those words flow freely out of their mouths because I cannot fathom a time where saying *colored people* over *African Americans* or *Black people* ever seemed like a plausible choice. I recall one incident after I sent a generic message out to my students regarding "language" after reading the word *colored* in a discussion post. I immediately received an e-mail request for a call from the student who happened to be an older white woman. She called because she wanted to present to me why she felt that she had a right to use the language and how not letting her speak in the way that she wants to will make her feel limited. I informed her that I, in no way, intend to limit her being able to engage in class but under no circumstance could I allow for her or anyone else to use harmful language and not address it. The student went on to tell me about how she married her husband so he could get a green card etc. What I would love for white people to understand is that the way that you all choose to relate to us in most cases is completely unnecessary and inappropriate. Please, stop it.

The conversation continued with the student letting me know that she was older than me and had served in the military as if that was supposed to stamp her worldview. I sincerely think that there is a disconnect in how white people understand the concept of race discourse and appropriateness which is an absolute choice. Using the excuse that people are older and set in their ways or "during my time" as a rationalization for your continued perpetuation of harm or for many of you to be complicit because you do not want to upset dinner to disrupt them is wack. Part of being a person on a journey toward anti-racism as a white person means that you have to stand up even when it is most uncomfortable and the person that you are redirecting is a revered elder. You cannot ever truly be on a journey toward anti-racism as a white person if you legitimately believe only the people that you dislike or that are your peers are deserving of a redirect. If you operate in that regard, then you have a lot more work to do in understanding what it means to be thoroughly anti-racist. In order for us to stop the mental, physical, and emotional murders of the marginalized by white people of all ilk's then we need all of you to get really comfortable with being uncomfortable.

ARE WE EVER REALLY SAFE IN WHITE SPACES?

The short and sweet answer is, no! A unique experience that African Americans and other folks of color have is that *if* we are self-aware, we exist in a constant state of knowing. Knowing that at any moment in time that white supremacy in some variation could absolutely come for you. The sometimes-difficult part of it all is finding the capacity to settle yourself in joy which is very intentional work. As a result of white supremacy and in white spaces in particular there is always an air of uneasiness that many of us feel because you are looking for your sense of belonging as well as sameness with colleagues across the institution or perhaps on another campus close by. When I arrived in Texas in 2020 during the height of the pandemic, I was reasonably terrified. For starters, Texas was *never* on my to-do-list of places that I wanted to live and couple that with how their elected officials chose to politicize the pandemic I was not a fan. It was not until I arrived on campus when I realized that Texas was an open carry state. Although North Carolina was also an open carry state I can assure you that Charlotte and the DFW are two vastly different places. When I would go to Walmart, I would see people open carrying as if they were waiting for something to jump off in the milk aisle. I very quickly limited my trips to Walmart and opted for Target or simply order what I needed and had it delivered. Yes, I know those are not the preferred Texas grocers like H-E-B, Sprouts, or WinCo but it was what I knew and what made me feel safer.

The adjustment was one that I could not fully prepare for because of all the places that I have lived it was the first place that made me feel like I was no longer in the United States. The energy was very different, and the racism was omnipresent. Do not get me wrong when I speak of my experience in Texas because in spite of the hellscape that it was I met some forever people! My arrival in Texas was one full of firsts because I was becoming the first African American or anyone to be in a joint appointment between two vastly different departments. One of the appointments was poised to allow this very work that I do to have a home. The other appointment was situated in quieting who I am, the work that I do, and hell bent on forcing me to play small. At times, they both operated in the same way in their attempts to humble and even humiliate me. I endured this treatment because it was by no small feat that I was able to land an academic job amid a global pandemic and in particular at a Research 1 university.

I suffered, and what is the craziest part about it all is that I still thrived professionally. This is the part of our experiences that Black people often talk about. The invisibility of our labor and the invisibility of our pain. I was winner of a Black faculty excellence award, and I was still being bullied pretty regularly. I often felt like I had nowhere to turn because not all of the Black people who were in my proximity were disruptors and many of them were just attempting to avoid becoming the targets themselves, so I get it. hooks taught us that the academy was certainly no paradise but what the academy does do is provide a space where learning can occur and that learning can feel like paradise is possible (Ohito and Brown 2021). I enjoyed being with my students and in the moments when I was able to enjoy community with a select few other Black faculty and staff at the university, I felt like I could just be. Those moments were short lived and often few and far between. The violence was so bad that I felt like the only way that I could survive living there was to actually get out of Texas. I would fly back to DC at least once a month when my schedule permitted to see my sister, close relatives, fraternity brothers, and friends. They would help me to fill my cup and each time would send me back to Texas feeling loved, supported, and purposed. I truly love my people more than these words could ever say. I am thankful for them because they always make me feel possible. Many people outside of the academy do not understand what it takes for Black people to exist inside of it or that we in fact need those Black people to be able to exist in it.

It is important that we are able to be a guide for Black students coming up behind us to show them that they are also possible. As Ohito & Brown (2021) posit, PWIs are indeed white spaces, which like all spaces are governed by rules that are both explicit and implicit. Those rules are steeply rooted in anti-Black rhetoric and the politics of exclusion. As academics who strive to be at anti-racist PWIs are spaces that are intended for you and because of that intent it allows for you to be able to build coalitions and wield whatever power given to you to be a beacon for equitable change. Far too often I have white people ask myself and other critical scholars what they can do. If I am honest, I find that question to be draining because it feels lazy and unvetted.

You all are privy to certain conversations and know full well when certain things are in motion aimed at harming Black men and women in your departments. You look at them every day and smile in their face and yet you say nothing. *Why?* Telling us after the harm is done how sorry you are or offering your assistance after the harm feels a bit performative and counterproductive. Do more and say more and say it to the people who are the power playing decision makers. We do not need to or care to see you crying about our harm when you have the ability or access to stop it. In addition, do not bring people of color into environments that you know will not be welcoming to them. You cannot claim to be innocent in the perpetuation of anti-Blackness if you know your institution is not situated to properly uplift, nurture, and support Black folks and folks of color. Stop the performative DEI recruitment and actually do the work in turning your departments and institutions around so they are actually places where people who are not white and male will actually thrive. The insidiousness of actual and metaphorical anti-Black violence is often manifested as absence and erasure of the people that you pretended to care about in the first place (Ohito and Brown 2021). The academy and many PWIs operate as a revolving door of intellectually exhausted Blackness because there will always be one of us assumably brought in to replace another of us without explanation. The tactics of the academy are so pervasively anti-Black because as part of the explicit rules that we all understand as members within is that very similar to fight club you do not talk about the academy. We are taught not to buck the system or fight back until we earn tenure and then once most folks earn tenure, they become complicit in the continued perpetuation of the harm. I cannot speak for anyone else but that is one condition of the academy that I cannot and will not agree to.

A resounding and residual experience of Black people in the academy is the surprise of anti-Black racism almost immediately upon your arrival. It is almost as if PWIs put their most horrible of people under hypnosis during your entire interview process for fear that perhaps you could change your mind. There must be a bat signal that goes out once the ink is dried on your contract and your final box is unpacked because in that moment *here comes the boom* or whatever DMX said. The disrespect and anti-Blackness begins almost right away and only stops once you leave or another person comes in and is able to share in the violent load. If you ever want to know how violent an institution is, find a Black woman and ask her. When I first arrived at my former institution, I remember feeling completely isolated in my split appointment which was partially in the Criminology department. I was largely disappointed in all of the Black folks because I was younger than all of them and I moved across the country alone. I was hopeful that they would gather together and brief me on the *ins and outs* of the department and who to watch out for. Interestingly enough, all but one of them provided the exact same name of the person who I should always be mindful of. I knew that they were telling the truth because they all operated differently within the department and had no reason to lie since they had nothing to gain by telling me. I remained cordial with the person but never let my hair down around them. If I have learned anything substantial in life it is to always believe what Black women tell you.

Black women are uniquely positioned to be the first to feel the disrespect and the stain of anti-Blackness in any white space. I remember all of the anti-Trump conversations from a few of the white folks in my department and the main one to espouse his rhetoric most often was the most paternalistic toward me. Liberal white supremacists are not likely to be the ones who pulled up to DC and wrote on the walls of the Capitol (Jones 2022). However, they are absolutely the ones who will remind you that you are to remain beneath them and will work overtime making sure that you do not forget it. "Liberal" racists are some of the worst offenders of anti-Blackness because they feel that since they are anti-Trump that somehow makes them different from those other white people. Fam, if you have not disrupted the hold that white supremacy has on your life you will act just like those people except that you have faux progressive leaning politics in the daytime. The most dangerous side of this benevolence is found in the workplace where it intentionally targets Black folks and primarily Black women (Jones 2022). One day I was told by one of my former department heads that he would be surprised if I was not poached by another university before my first year concluded because I was that dope. A few months passed and he saw how already connected I was and how things were happening for me rather quickly and he then tried to place a seed of doubt in my capability of landing at a more known Research 1 university.

This conversation was happening as I was on the east coast, in a hotel room, and watching how one of my own tweets became a story about the Georgetown professor who had been fired for being racist. The conversation could not have been more ridiculous, and I felt like I was having one of those fourth wall breaking moments like Gregory Eddie on *Abbott Elementary*. That call was sadly from a person who was tenured and looked like me. The sad part about it all is that I wish I could say that I was the only one in all of the world who ever had to experience this, but it unfortunately would not be true. In my very millennial way, I believe that I bucked the system in the best ways that I could. I am always respectful to people in authority roles, deferential even. But what I am absolutely not, nor will I ever be is a punching bag for anyone in the academy. I do not care about my role in the academy that much to not let it be known about how you *will* handle and address me. I believe that is something that later born Gen-Xers, Millennials, and Gen-Z academics have in common and that is that we are willing to do the work, but we are not willing to be bullied while we do it.

The *fuck this place* vibe sits squarely on my tongue ready to be fully executed when and if ever needed. White supremacy exists as an institutional system of power that privileges, normalizes, and maintains whiteness and white advantages in all aspects of life including higher education (Bell et al. 2021). White supremacy exists in this way because it has no fear of the majority beneficiaries ever declining their investment in it. The academy and liberal politics are full of aversive racists who are people who actually believe themselves to be anti-racist while still harboring negative attitudes and feelings about minoritized group members [*namely African Americans*] (Bell et al. 2021). No one wants to be labeled a racist, but everyone wants the freedom to be racist. *How?!*

MARTHA! GRAB YOUR SENSIBLE SHOES!

It is time for you to roll your sleeves up and to get involved. Use your body, use your wallet, and use your access to assist in the collective fight for liberation. The time is now, and you are needed. Before you hop in the streets make sure you have on your sensible shoes because it might get a little rough around here. The first thing you need to do is to make sure that you check yourself for your own biases. Not just today as we take to the streets but everyday for the rest of your natural life. Are there certain members of marginalized groups that bother you? Perhaps they are the members of said group who chose pluralism over assimilation and that somehow conflicts with your own views of socially acceptable belonging. Are you sitting in judgement of the Black woman who came outside with her comfortable clothes because she was running behind and wanted to make the meeting or are you just glad that she showed up to discuss how to best assist her child?

As you begin to understand more intentionally about the mattering of Black Lives how do you now understand how Blue Lives, All Lives, and whatever else is rooted in white supremacy? Calling them ignorant and or foolish does not go far enough and it blames the ills of their intention on a condition of which they have no control. Racist white people absolutely with every fiber of their being mean each and everything that they say or do. They are only apologetic and teary eyed when they realized that the privilege of their whiteness *might* not work this time. How are you prepared to have the difficult conversation and how do you maintain the integrity of the conversation when the audience that you are engaging with tries to derail the conversation with statements like *what about Black-on-Black crime?!* In what ways are you prepared to support abolition? How might you understand abolition in the contemporary context? Which Black intersectional feminists are you reading and how do they guide your understanding of how you step up and or aside as needed? How are you cultivating a space of authentic acceptance in your place of work and being intentional about supporting Black folks? In what ways do you see yourself able to move out the toxic old guard who do not wish to see a place where all people of color are welcomed and supported? How have you poised yourself to be rejected by some Black folks who have been burned enough and do not wish to be aligned with you and still stay in the fight? This is not the moment where you say *welp, I tried* and then go back to being a performing liberal. Do you think you have 500 years' worth of patience? I hope so because if you are serious about this you will need it. How are you reconstructing your curriculum to not only read our work but to invite us into the space for true engagement and *then* paying us. *How?*

In what ways have you poised yourself to understand that the absence of race in a conversation about policies and institutional changes means that racism is loudly centered in the conversation? Understanding that your challenging of white supremacy and anti-Black rhetoric must start within you and always be internal. Racialized categories within the United States are grounded in how white people see themselves in comparison to the marginalized (Curry and Curry 2018). What is your relationship with white supremacy? Please understand that saying that you do not have a relationship with white supremacy is absolutely not the correct answer. I do not wish to provide you a space of avoidance and apathy to the real harm that is anti-Black racism and white supremacy. As such, I must insist that you wrestle with what your relationship has been, is, and what it will be in relationship to the anti-racist [*co-conspirator*] journey you are opting to take part in. How are you planning to facilitate discourse with your family, friends, and perhaps lover who does not agree with your sentiment and believes that it is a bunch of *ado* about nothing? I hate to break the news to you, but you cannot be in a true relationship with someone who opposes anti-racism if you are committed to living your life in such a way. I know your family told you never to discuss such things over your casserole, but I am here to confirm and affirm for you that somebody lied! You absolutely must engage anyone you plan to share intimate space with about where they are in their journey, or their racist rhetoric will eventually encapsulate your own.

For many of the people in your spheres who consider themselves to be good, conflict avoidant, non-racist, or anti-Black-Black folks they wish to insist that the only race is the human race (Curry and Curry 2018). This is called avoidance and it is racism. The core of race neutrality asserts that while class, gender, and race may in fact provide differences between physical bodies the human essence is beneath it all and must be the only focus (Curry and Curry 2018). This ideology disallows for accountability and responsibility to exist especially if people who espouse it in the next breath refer to themselves as white and me as Black or use the n-word if they become angry enough. A great deal of the people who claim to be race neutral are most certainly part of the 74,223,975 people who voted for the twice impeached president in 2020. For this reason, you must be direct in your discourse regarding race and racism to truly be considered a co-conspirator in the fight for Black liberation.

REFERENCES

Bell, Myrtle P., Daphne Berry, Joy Leopold, and Stella Nkomo. 2021. "Making Black Lives Matter in academia: A Black feminist call for collective action against anti-blackness in the academy." *Gender Work Organ,28 (S1)* 39–57.

Curry, Tommy J., and Gwenetta Curry. 2018. "On the Perils of Race Neutrality and Anti-Blackness: Philosophy as an Irreconcilable Obstacle to (Black) Thought." *The American Journal of Economics and Sociology, Vol 77. Nos.3–4* 657–687.

Jones, Jaye. 2022. "The Banality of Liberal White Supremacy: Black Women leaders, Administrative Marginalization, and the Professional Toll of Anti-Blackness." *Dialogues in Social Justice: An Adult Education Journal, Vol. 7 No.1* 1–10.

Ohito, Esther O., and Keffrelyn D. Brown. 2021. "Feeling safe from the storm of anti-Blackness: Black affective networks and the im/possibility of safe classroom spaces in Predominantly White Institutions." *Curriculum Inquiry, Vol. 51. No.1* 135–160.

Watson, Teri N., and Gwendolyn S. Baxley. 2021. "Centering 'Grace': Challenging Anti-Blackness in Schooling Through Motherwork." *Journal of School Leadership,Vol 31. (1–2)* 142–157.

Chapter 8

Freedom

Self-Liberation

FREEDOM! FREEDOM! WHERE ARE YOU?!

Freedom is a right granted by birth, but freedom has always been used as a bargaining tool of oppression by white supremacy. The oppressors of Blackness have created every possible way to dangle freedom in our faces like a carrot. Freedom seems like an unimaginable concept and has caused many members of marginalized groups to become disenfranchised or forces a mindset of "settling." *Beyoncé'* and *Kendrick Lamar*'s anthem reminds us to continue to run and fight to break our own chains. The fight for liberation means that we must first fight to free ourselves and then work as a collective to free everyone else. Black liberation includes the liberation of all Black people, and it is not based upon the condition of cishetero-normativity, class, educational attainment, or social status and privilege. *Everybody!*

To be a descendant of enslaved Africans in this country is bittersweet. By bittersweet I mean that I am in no way ashamed of them or my lineage, but I feel a profound sadness when I consider what they endured. To exist in a country for centuries and still have no idea who the earliest people in your bloodline are is humiliating and demoralizing and that was the intent. White people having the ability to own our personal histories and then passing legislation to say that we cannot legally learn about it is another form of enslavement. The rage that I feel as white supremacists pass laws that will never directly impact them and then silencing our queries about reparations is a special kind of hell that only the members of Native Nations could also comprehend. We are the only group of Black people within this country who are African by blood and American by force. We are largely disqualified from claiming any relation to Africa because many of us do not know from where we hail. We are also not able to fully benefit at large from the social experiment that is America because white people have positioned themselves to be the deciders of who among us will make it. Whiteness still operates in relationship to Blackness in a paternalistic form. It shows up in most ways that white people think displays *allyship* or as proof of their anti-racism. As an example, when you, a white teacher, decide that you would like to teach in the hood [*by way of TFA or some other educational scam*] because you believe that the students of color could benefit from your "unique" insight. It was also displayed at the height of the pandemic when Congress decided to give [*eligible**] Americans $1,200 on two different occasions. But wait, it gets worse! The former President had to make sure that it was his signature that appeared on the check which made people believe that it was his decision. It was also the way that wealthy white people debated about the $1,200 as if that was enough money to lift the oppressed out of poverty. *It was absurd!* But for some people the bait and switch worked! We began seeing debates on Black Twitter about how much DJT had done for African Americans and I began thinking that I was losing it. *He did what?! And for who?!*

I think as New Yorkers we had a more accurate depiction of who he and the former NYC mayor turned election denier were. We did not need to see January 6th, the "Four Seasons," or the stolen documents at Mar-a-Lago to know that there was absolutely foolishness amok. The gift of whiteness is that it makes other white people pretend to forget just how awful some of their comrades are. I will never forget about or forgive DJT for begging New York State to bring back the death penalty so Black and Latinx youth could be murdered, and I will never forgive those who supported his election as a result. I will never forget about *stop and frisk* and what that did to a generation of that same youth demographic. Conveniently forgetting about the dangers of whiteness and white supremacy because of $1,200 is deadly. Having said that, I can also acknowledge the full privilege of my mindset and being aware of who I am in my body as to not be easily swayed or misled by whiteness in any capacity. Fully understanding the complexity of the Black living condition and why $1,200 was a lifesaver for many I want us to know that we are owed a lot more than $1,200 and that it is because of that same version of white supremacy that you needed the $1,200 anyway. As a result of so many of us not fully knowing who we are we constantly find ourselves embattled in social media incited diaspora wars. I am still not sure if many of us know that most of those arguments are started by bots and white men and women in Twitter blackface. White supremacy has created what feels like a forever separation between us and our distant relatives from our motherland and her daughter countries. The violence of white supremacy is that in order to carry out its actions a person does not have to be white. White supremacy is the seed and any living being or institutional entity can carry out its mission.

Liberating ourselves means being clear on who the enemy has always been, and that the enemy should never be other Black people. Although each of our

Black lived experiences are unique, they are also ours and ours alone. Our liberation should not ever hinge upon meeting the approval of the white gaze. Self-liberation is essential to understanding how we as a people can move forward and legitimately take our place in the sun unencumbered by whiteness. I always ask my students questions that ignite a deeper analysis of thought. One of the more recent questions was *what did you see your role in the fight for liberation as?* I ask this because I want to make it plain that this fight, this everyday fight, is not the sole responsibility of the marginalized who did not choose to have their lives *othered.* Most of my students feel hopeless and say things like *it would be too hard because there are more of them.* The feeling of hopelessness in the fight against white supremacy is a feeling all too common for many but as I told them anything that can be dreamed can be achieved. There are lots of ways that we assist in feeding the cancer of white supremacy and if we start with our own self-work we can begin to eat away at the success and reach of white supremacy.

Freedom, Cut Me Loose!

One of the greatest liberatory gifts you must give yourself is divesting away from white supremacy. *Yes!* I am telling you to end the relationship that you have with white supremacy. It is the only true way to free *both* yourself and others. Many African Americans [*and most Americans actually*] are not remotely aware of what white supremacy is in full form. Most of us believe that white supremacy is always something that you can see, touch, and therefore immediately notice. Part of understanding your relationship to white supremacy is to begin by understanding your relationship to *preferences* and how you arrived there. Through our relationship with religiosity, we are forced into codes that disallows for us to allow the full human condition of others to take shape or exist in proximity to us. You might even feel like you can catch whatever "the thing" is that you are so adamantly opposed to. Perhaps, you are already living with and within "the thing" and you have not allowed yourself the freedom of self-expression to fully understand who you are. And guess what? That is absolutely your choice to reside in the prison that you have created for yourself. But what is not okay? Is you then using that same logic to force others who are freely expressive to do that too.

What is "the thing" that I am speaking of? It could be the one specific thing that is jumping around in your mind as you read this, or it could be any number of things that you oppose for your own *Godly* reasons. As a result of white supremacy, we are trained to believe that there is only one version of Blackness that we must all adhere to, or risk being ostracized. I think that the respectable crew annoy me just as much as the homophobic crew because I find them both to be the most insolent. Placing yourself on some moral high ground simply because the dirt that you do is less visible is so *churchy* that it makes me itch. Where is your spiritual alignment and why is that not centered over a fine representation of prudish behavior which is actually rooted in envy? You might find yourself to be envious because deep down in you there is a person who wishes they had the courage to be as brazen as other folks are. White supremacy has trapped you into thinking that only you and people like you deserve to exist. My counter point is that you deserve to exist *and* people who are nothing like you deserve to exist too. What does not deserve to exist are the anti-Black thoughts that you have as a result of your differences. When we allow anti-Blackness to proliferate in every space that we inhabit [*by our own hands*] we invite in suffering and select traumas of the psychological, physical, and the intellectual kind (Griffin and Turner 2021). We then pass those very problematic perspectives onto youth and force them to internalize their Blackness as something that must be tolerated as opposed to something that deserves to simply, *be*.

Who would you have been if you did not limit yourself? What did you tell yourself that you were incapable of accomplishing? And then ask yourself who was the person that initially stirred up those deficit thoughts within you. I can guarantee that the biases that you now hold onto like a child death grip did not start out that way. Someone within your sphere introduced that hate to you and on this day and in this moment, I am granting you permission to let it go. Let go of the false pretenses and the interpretations of yourself as needing to be perfect to have the right to exist. Do this for you so that you can then allow that same space for someone else to be released too. Give yourself permission to move from *pessimism* to *optimistic realism*. We understand that our living condition in America is absolutely marred by the period of enslavement and white supremacy (Griffin and Turner 2021). However, that does not mean that you have to continue to live within the context of Blackness that has been forced upon you regardless of how safe it makes them feel. Whiteness does not ever make me feel safe at any place and at any time and I have not once ever heard a white person tell the other people to tone their whiteness down, to be a little less white, or to keep that white ghetto shyt at home. So, why do *you* do it for them? Why is their safety and belonging more important than yours or your people?

Although the physical manifestation of enslavement is no longer with most of us there are still absolutely aspects of our minds and spirits that are still heavily shackled (Griffin and Turner 2021). In a class discussion, a student asked *what do you do when people refuse to acknowledge the realities of racism?* I said to the student that their confirmation of what I already know is a burden too heavy for me to carry. I wish not to make my words change the minds of those too stubborn to realize that they are wrong. I spend none of my time with those people and I care not to. I will only invest time in engaging with people who might be unaware and are still early in their journeys toward anti-racism but are open to learning. I also told that same student that everyone cannot go. What I mean by that is if we spend all of our energy in trying to convince people who have already made their minds up that white supremacy and anti-Blackness are essential then we cannot invest our good energy in helping the people who need us in their journey toward healing. If you are knee-deep in the weeds of trying to convince those individuals, you are wasting everyone's time and mainly your own. All you are responsible for is giving the people access to the information and not keeping it to yourself, but you cannot force people to engage with it, so stop trying to.

The history of this country is situated in Black degradation in order to keep colonial order and this is represented within institutions of higher learning, society at large, and in our relationships with whiteness (Dancy II, Edward and Davis 2018). Essentially white supremacy and upholding it does not need your help it seems to be doing just fine. Anti-Blackness is situated in understanding that it allows us [*the descendants of the enslaved*] not to be considered relational to humanity but as *forever property* (Dancy II et al. 2018). And for this reason and with that understanding years ago I vowed to never participate in it. People often get upset with me when they tell me things that are rooted in anti-Blackness that they consider a preference and I disagree with them and tell them that they are inherently anti-Black. Black folks respond to being called anti-Black in the same way that white folks respond to being called racist. Again, I do not understand being madder at people for naming the ways in which you are operating rather than divesting away from the named behavior. *The math isn't mathing!* In the context and with the full understanding of white supremacy and anti-Blackness as on brand for the way racist white people [*Republicans and Democrats alike*] act toward African Americans it is because we remain [*in their opinion*] the property of white people (Dancy II et al. 2018). Although our "freedom" has been legally granted we are still treated as property whether or not someone owns us. That alone should be enough to make you quickly break up with how safe you go out of your way to make white people feel. *Free yourself!*

I Break Chains All by Myself

I consider myself to be a disruptor of oppressive systems because I learned long ago that being enslaved to them does not work for me or for my people. When I was a child, I would hear adults make smart comments about me being *mouthy.* What I can now say to those people is that I, in some metaphysical way, always knew who I was destined to be. I always knew how I was to be handled by people and I wish that confidence that shows up in little Black children be allowed to enter full bloom and that it not be stifled out by people who lost their own light. My people dislike mouthy children because it means that they will never be able to harm that child and not face accountability. I wish more children had the innate gift to be mouthy in some way and that the gift of mouthiness would be able to protect them from hurt, harm, and danger. I wish that more of us knew that we deserve to be as free as the little Black children before they enter the educational system where their spirits are ultimately broken (Love 2016; Engram 2022). If we were ever to maintain that level of self-actualization throughout our lives before white supremacy and anti-Black racism showed up and immediately began causing us to second guess who we are. Perhaps if this were what we instilled in our youth they would be prepared to respond when their white teachers inevitably tell them that being a lawyer, doctor, or graphic designer were too lofty of a goal and that perhaps they should consider manual labor roles. There is absolutely nothing wrong with those who manually labor but please be clear that it should be something that they selected for themselves based on their own natural skills. Not because they were taught by the educational system that anything else that they can imagine for themselves was impossible.

It truly lifts my heart when the random Instagram reel pops into my feed where it shows a Black father or mother pouring powerfully Black affirmation into their babies. Those affirmations are cute and adorable now but when those babies are fully grown those beautiful affirmations will become their life mantras. *I am beautiful. I am capable. I am deserving of love. I can do anything that I can dream of. I am necessary. I AM POSSIBLE!* Each of these are not only lessons for our babies but they are also lessons in learning to love *and* liberate ourselves. A freedom of choice and a freedom without permission from whiteness. Laying claim to your own soul and how you feed it is a blessing and a responsibility not to be taken lightly. Give yourself permission to be free and in that moment you also give other people permission to be free too. In one breath many of us will say that Blackness is not monolithic while enforcing Black codes of conduct upon our people that are situated in the permissions of whiteness. You are so concerned about being an embarrassment to people who see no issue with harassing Black children, mocking differently abled people, and walking on the back of the shoes of their colleagues at the Capitol because they dislike them. You seek the permission and respect of people who act like the worst versions of children and I simply cannot fathom why that is. *Let it go!* Give yourself permission to be Black AF and no that does not mean loud and belligerent. It simply means give yourself permission to be the best version of yourself that makes you feel the most fulfilled and aligned with your spirit.

We are a resilient people and have made great strides toward re-envisioning our relationship to our Blackness and all that we imagine it to be. Our ability to turn water into wine has always bothered our oppressors because short of physically killing us they could never master how to destroy our collective spirit. Our awakening and movement toward Black consciousness in the 60s helped us to shed calling ourselves names like "negro" which was also affixed to us by racist white people (Watson 2022). One of the greatest hopes of white supremacy is to make sure that Blackness is devalued throughout time (Watson 2022). Sit with this thought for just a moment. The people who tried to destroy you and your entire families existence are the same people who you prefer to perform for. Having a relationship with people who are racialized as white is not the same thing as having an intimate relationship with whiteness. You can absolutely be friends with people racialized as white without ever feeling the need to diminish or dismantle your Blackness to be among them. The performance is the thing I mentioned about Ronnie previously. Teaching Black people to love ourselves is not only a liberatory act of love it is also an act of resistance. This self-love is essential and necessary as a means of self-affirmation and survival particularly for us, a people too often unloved (Kirkland 2021).

In order for us to focus on loving and liberating ourselves an exercise in naming must also occur (Kirkland 2021). This exercise assists in unmasking the Black self, as to recover it, and to care for it (Kirkland 2021). A great deal of the harm that we inflict upon ourselves is because we never truly learned how to love ourselves and in turn we never learned how to properly love each other. We deal with each other in ways that cut deep and are at times unrepairable because we did not know how to communicate our own pain. A practice that I try my hardest to implement is to fight about *the thing* and in fighting about *the thing* I do not swing below the belt in relationships. For me, this is a radical act of love because in any fight that you participate in the goal is to win. However, when you do things with and in love the goal should never be to win the goal should be to learn and hear. When I talk to my friends who might be experiencing difficulty in their relationships I remind them to fight only about *the thing* and never to fight dirty or personal. Teaching ourselves how to operate in love is not only radical it for many is seemingly impossible. It is seemingly impossible because for many of us love is relegated *only* to intimate connections not connections within our community, and they are wrong.

We must teach ourselves to move beyond self-serving love. A love that is only given out when and if it serves you. Moving through life only looking out for yourself is a condition developed within you because of all of the loss suffered during enslavement. Many of our ancestors were taken away from their families at early ages and sent only God knows where, where they might be lucky if the elders at their new location looked after them. Some of them were fortunate because of the gracious *othermothers* and some were left to take care of themselves. That trauma is passed directly through DNA and it presents in each of us today. You have to stop the passing of that trauma by healing yourself from it. Naming race and racism as paramount to why we operate in the broken ways that we do is necessary to create a space for healing. If you cannot name your harm you cannot begin to move toward reconciling and commanding that harm. Naming it is critical to the dialectic of learning and teaching, because in the lives of Black folks, neither education or socio-historical experiences are universal or neutral (Kirkland 2021). *Name it!* Unnaming race and racism and allowing it to exist in as Toni Morrison calls "the *dark*" giving it permission to continue and to exist (Kirkland 2021). We are aiming to usher out the ability to do harm to us in the shadows and continuing to make us feel that the harm is our own doing. What the Governor of Florida is currently doing is because folks have refused to name it. His actions are racist and there should be no deciphering of it in any other way. We must all remain courageous enough to fight for our freedom and to dream up liberation as impossible as it sometimes seems (Kirkland 2021). The hardest part of the fight for liberation is continuing to in spite of all that takes place, believe. The belief is where the unimaginable can occur. Think about all of the things that you have accomplished in your life whatever they might be. Did they not all begin with a dream? A dream that you willed yourself to believe were possible and attainable.

'CAUSE A WINNER DON'T QUIT ON THEMSELVES

Sometimes we have to give ourselves space to allow the kid that lives within each of us to run wild. If you still have living parents or elders who were around during your developmental years you should ask them how you were. *What sorts of things did you bring up? What were your dreams at that age? Who and what did you want to be? What inspired you?* Asking these questions will allow for you to be able to reconnect with the part of you that you lost sight of. In conversations with my mom I often ask her, other than being a mother figure, what is it that she wants to be. Sadly, when my mom describes the things that she wants to be she always begins by describing herself as being in service of others. I wonder how many other Black women always think about themselves not as whole people and individuals but as servants to others. I push harder, and harder, because I try to break through to see if she can remember what her original *why* was and perhaps how she lost it. When I think of my mom and what I hope she thinks of herself as is someone who was a whole person before she was a mother. Someone who can still be a whole person even after becoming a mother. Most importantly, I hope that she sees her dreams as possible and through her own eyes, not the eyes of others. Our dreams for ourselves once we become full fledged adults have to supersede anyone else's dreams and interpretations of us.

The American educational system has greatly contributed to the Black sense of worthlessness (Kirkland 2021). Our experiences within the schooling system in the United States as African Americans has been one deeply rooted in spirit breaking and oppression. They were oppressive not only because they operated like prisons but they were oppressive because we were locked into white concepts of ourselves. My senior year I recall a massive sweep that pushed several of our classmates out of school as a result of truancy and aging out. I actually recall someone in one of my classes my senior year who was actually twenty years old. I did think that he was old as hell then but I never really interrogated why. I do briefly recall a story where he told me that he lived in Europe for a year and worked at H&M. This was right around the time that H&M was making its way into malls in the United States. I never thought much more beyond that but I am sure that he had a difficult life experience that would have led him to make such a drastic move as a high schooler. He went on to join the military and we keep in touch via Facebook from time-to-time.

I attended what was referred to as an "inner city" school and I remember we had this slogan on our t-shirts that we wore with our track and field uniforms. The slogan was *F.I.C.A.* which stood for focused inner city athlete and we wore those shirts often without a second thought. I am cringing as I sit here and reflect on it because I am recognizing that it was in response to the suburban schools anti-Black response toward us. Even in our moments of joy we still were forced to perform for whiteness. I guess that was their way of saying that we [*the athletes*] were less dangerous and more respectable than perhaps our "less focused" non-athlete peers. Well-intentioned whiteness was always something that we had to combat and to rehash it is hilarious, enraging, and heartbreaking all at the same time.

In the scholars program that I was a member of there was one white woman who gave really terrible advice and they revolved around conflict. The first was about what to do once we became high schoolers in the event that an upperclassmen wanted to fight us. She told us to lay on the ground in the fetal position because that would let them know that we were harmless. *Bruh, hell nah!* When we were preparing to visit D.C. she told us not to make eye contact with people there because they were strangers and it could be dangerous. I am happy to report that I avoided the fetal position and the only time I have ever walked with my head down was when we visited a correctional facility for a criminal justice class in high school. *Yes, that happened too! In re*: white teachers. It is almost like they lose all of their good sense when they engage with non-white students and it is very-very weird. As Ladson-Billings taught us in her approach to teaching being culturally relevant and that the ways that we teach must be framed around cultural framings and center that relate to the learners (Kirkland 2021). They took us on a field trip to a minimum security prison and I am wondering what part of my culture that experience was supposed to be centered around and connected to.

We need less prison visits and more engaging the needs of the students from their own cultural framing and not the one that the random white teacher believes it should be. I cannot fathom how taking us to a prison or telling us to lay in fetal position affirmed either our Blackness or our humanity in any way. The ever present reminder of anti-Black racism is resonant in how we view ourselves because of politics, economic structures, and education within our bodies (Rogers, Versey and Cielto 2021). Those moments that I previously mentioned never caused me to have a negative depiction of myself because I was affirmed within my family in various ways. With this consideration I certainly cannot speak for what those experiences did for my peers because we are all individuals with shared and individualized lived experiences. I like to think that I was laser focused and aware of what I was intended to do and I would like to say that most of my friends were too. Life just took shape differently for us and for multiple reasons. When I think about the weight of white criticism and what it does to us as people although I do not have children of my own, I do have nieces and nephews who I am a father figure for. I often think about them and how they see themselves in the world as result of their experiences with white supremacy. I only hope that they have enough positive affirmations around them that are enough to combat the darkness of anti-Black racism externally and internally.

As indicated by the work of Matsuda in the 80s understanding how we [*the marginalized*] tell our versions of our stories is key [*counternarratives*] because through us the world can have a better understanding of life in the United States and all that it encompasses (Kinloch, Penn and Burkhard 2020). Naming, storying, and counternarratives also provides us a way of knowing for ourselves as well guiding the youth through their journey of understanding anti-Blackness as well as white supremacy. The truth is that for the marginalized racism does not wait until we are age appropriate and able to defend ourselves. As soon as racism has an opportunity to latch onto us it absolutely will. Many of us experienced anti-Black racism as we journeyed earthside in our mother's womb and as a result of that same reason some of us did not make it earth side and we took our mother's with us.

STOLE FROM ME, LIED TO ME, NATION HYPOCRISY

As aspirational as the *kumbaya* chorus is for some people before I can ever imagine a racial reconciliation I must first imagine our liberation. Some people might read that and say that reconciliation must happen before liberation and I fundamentally disagree. As always, asking us to reconcile a relationship that we never agreed to is violent as hell particularly when the other party claims no responsibility. Our homeland was stolen from us, our names were stolen from us, our language was stolen from us, and all we have to show for it are contemporary versions of oppression but designer. Lynching just became federally illegal in 2022 and five states just voted to abolish slavery in November of 2022. *In 2022!* The assumption that we should even consider bending more toward reconciliation when the beneficiaries of whiteness have not even attempted to meet us halfway is offensive. Our liberation is not something that we are willing to negotiate about because it is ours for the taking and our patience in this regard is because we are a peaceful people.

A resistance that is formed as a direct result of oppression is also shaped by it (Haynes, et al. 2019). As Nikole Hannah-Jones argued in 2019, America [*gestures wildly*] was never a democracy until WE made it one. Many of us have given so much of ourselves out of a sense of loyalty to this country. I am reminded of the countless soldiers who gave their lives for this country because the promise of freedom seemed so sweet. Knowing the desperation that weighed on our ancestors as they simply tried to figure out the best way to exist in this country amid their captors and the constant denial is gut wrenching. Black men were threatened for wearing their uniforms in public and accused of having a carnal lust for white women because it was rumored that they had enjoyed their fair share of them during the World War. With no real proof of anything white people per usual set out to make the lives of Black veterans a living hell. My family has a long storied history with the military since my dad, uncles, and a host of cousins are veterans and had they been born just twenty years earlier they could have been either of those lynched men. America has an uncanny way of always reminding Black people of their place as property and as a colonized people.

We have always been loyal to the bright stripes and the bright stars and they have never been loyal to us. *Ever!* Regardless of all that we have endured in this country there is a belief that there should be no end to that loyalty and that for me is a wild ass concept. Any Black person who is blindly patriotic without critique is a Black person that concerns me. African Americans have always been foundational to the democracy of America (Hannah-Jones 2019). Even when our participation in the democratic aspects of this country hinges upon whether or not white people believe that we deserve it. This country was built on our literal backs and our blood stains the soil but none of that has ever been enough. White people always want more from us all while terrorizing us. Where is the limit? A country built upon oppressing its people cannot simply move on. There absolutely must be a resolve and a halting to any further violating of the oppressed.

The United States and white people have received way too many concessions for their role in the creation of race, white supremacy, racism, and enslavement. It is the only crime that everyone knows about but no one does anything about it. White supremacy is an actual crime against humanity and enslavement was mass genocide just as the holocaust was. The United States has made repair and paid reparations in several other instances with communities that it has harmed and even paid reparations to our enslavers. As a matter of historical significance the United States has never apologized for or attempting to make amends for how slavery has shaped the lives of the descendants of the enslaved. The reason for this is because white people including our elected officials do not feel that we, the descendants of the enslaved, are deserving of anything, when the contrary is true. *We deserve everything!* The matter of reparations and whether or not African Americans are owed anything, much like masking and COVID, have become matters of political prudence. The matter remains that if the United States were to own their liability in the enslavement of our ancestors it would then open up the potential for additional lawsuits and as a matter of fact it should. The United States has been complicit in the continued oppression of the descendants of the enslaved as a result of the enslaving of our ancestors in the first place.

Asking white people what they think about the matter of reparations in public domain is a further slap to the face to our history in this country. White people are proud of their country, their privilege, and their ability to oppress us at all times. Do we legitimately expect people who voted for DJT twice to actually care about the repair of the descendants of the enslaved? *Be forreal!* I feel as strongly about this as I do about cisgender men having the right to opinions about women's reproductive health. And for the record, I believe that the only opinion that we should have is in support of minding our cis-male business. And that is a lesson that I believe white people should have in the matter of making us whole for what we have endured and continued to endure throughout history. *Freedom* is not only about our receiving justice. *Freedom* is also about us receiving our liberation and our reparations.

REFERENCES

Dancy II, T. Elon, Kirsten T. Edward, and James Earl Davis. 2018. "Historically White Universities and Plantation Politics: Anti-Blackness and Higher Education in the Black Lives Matter Era." *Urban Education,Volume 53, Issue 2* 176–195.
Engram Jr., Frederick V. 2022. "Who's All Over There? Patriarchy, White Manning, and Deficit Framed Thinking Aimed at Spirit Murdering Black Children, Vol. 18 No. 1." *International Forum of Teaching and Studies* 49–53.

Griffin, Autumn, and Jennifer Turner. 2021. "Toward a Pedagogy of Black Livingness: Black students' creative multimodal renderings of resistance to anti-Blackness." *English Teaching: Practice & Critique, Vol. 20 No. 4* 440–453.

Hannah-Jones, Nikole. 2019. "America Wasn't a Democracy, Until Black Americans Made It One." *New York Times.*

Haynes, Chayla, Milagros Castillo-Montoya, Meseret Hailu, and Saran Stewart. 2019. "Black Deprivation, Black Resistance, and Black Liberation: the influence of #BlackLivesMatter (BLM) on higher education." *International Journal of Qualitative Studies in Education,Vol. 32 No.9* 1067–1071.

Kinloch, Valarie, Carlotta Penn, and Tanja Burkhard. 2020. "Black Lives Matter: Storying, Identities, and Counternarratives." *Journal of Literacy Research,Volume 52, Issue 4* 382–405.

Kirkland, David E. 2021. "A Pedagogy for Black People: Why Naming Race Matters." *Equity & Excellence in Education, Vol. 54 No.1* 60–67.

Love, Bettina. 2016. "Anti-Black state violence, classroom edition: The spirit murdering of Black children, 13:1." *Journal of Curriculum and Pedagogy* 22–25.

Rogers, Leoandra Onnie, H. Shellae Versey, and Janene Cielto. 2021. "'They're Always Gonna Notice My Natural Hair': Identity, Intersectionality and Resistance Among Black Girls." *Quality Psychology* 1–21.

Watson, Marcus D. 2022. "White Supremacy's Horcrux and Why The Black Power Movement Almost Destroyed It." *Journal of African American Studies.*

Chapter 9

For Gianna

And All of the Children of the Stolen . . .

I pray for you.
I pray that, in spite of it all, that you have the support that you need.
I pray that, for all that the world made your dad (*Floyd*) out to be, that you hold his love for you in your secret place.
A place that only you can find.
A place that when you feel sad or lonely that only you can go.
I pray for you.
I pray that, you grow into the fullness of yourself and that you are loved and protected.
I pray that, when the world becomes cruel, and you are old enough to know what happened, that you find your joy in his laughter, his jokes, and his embrace.
I pray for you.
I pray that, as much as this world hates us, and although that hate killed your dad, that you know that they do not define you, or us.
I will always pray for you.
Pray for me too.

Chapter 10

For Us All

To the Children of Mother Africa

I love you immensely.
I love you even though at different times of my life you were unable
to love me back.
Your love for me was impossible because during those times you
could barely love yourself.
I love you immensely.
Even during the times when you are most difficult to love.
Your
Gender Wars
Your
Homophobia
Your
Colorism
Your
Patriarchy
Your
Misogynoir
All of these are learned behaviors taught to us by those who held
and hold us captive.
I love you immensely.
I love you enough to tell you when you are wrong.
I love you enough to hold you accountable.
I love you enough to tell you that I am proud of you.
I love you.
Even when the world tells us that we are undeserving of love.
When the world taught us to hate ourselves, I loved you.
I love you immensely.
But what I would love from you . . .
Is for you to love yourself, too.

Index

About the Author

Frederick V. Engram Jr. is an incoming assistant professor of higher education at Fairleigh Dickinson University who hails from Utica, New York. Dr. Engram is an award-winning educator and higher education scholar. His research focuses on understanding how African Americans make sense of their experiences with anti-Black racism in higher education as well as the criminal justice system. He was named to two inaugural *40 under 40* lists regarding his scholar activist work by his fraternity Alpha Phi Alpha Fraternity Inc., and his undergraduate alma mater, Johnson C. Smith University. Dr. Engram is a notable speaker who has delivered keynote lectures at several institutions across North America and is a *TEDx* speaker. Dr. Engram's public scholarship has appeared in *Diverse Issues in Higher Education, Blavity*, and *Forbes.*